"What Goes On In This House, Stays In This House!"

POETRY

Echoes From The Children
Whose "Tears" Are Never Seen
Whose "Cries" Are Never Heard

Published By
Milligan Books

Cover Design By
Icehill UltraMedia

Formatting By
AbarCo Business Services

By

Tammy Woodard Rivers

Copyright © 1998 by Tammy Woodard Rivers
Memphis, TN
All rights reserved
Printed and Bound in the United States of America

Published and Distributed by:
Milligan Books
an imprint of Professional Business Consultants
1425 W. Manchester, Suite B,
Los Angeles, California 90047
(213) 750-3592

First Printing, November 1998
10 9 8 7 6 5 4 3 2 1

ISBN 1- 881524-37-X

All rights reserved. No part of this book may be reproduced in whole or in part, in any form or by any means, electronic or mechanical, including photocopying, recording or by any information storage and retrieval system, without permission in writing from the author. Address inquires to *Milligan Books,* 1425 W. Manchester, Suite B, Los Angeles, California 90047, (323) 750-3592

Printed in the United States of America

ACKNOWLEDGMENTS

This book is dedicated to God and all of his children.

To the love of my life, my genie in his magic lamp, my husband for always believing in me and for standing by me through every storm.

To my children for being "pure inspiration and joy", but most of all, for just "being".

To my mother for being my mother and for feeding me my first spoonful of poetry.

To Lay for always being just a phone call away.

To Granddad for being my "perfect father".

To Dr. Rosie Milligan for encouraging me to turn a dream into a reality and for holding my hand and helping me to cross the finish line.

To James and Linda for helping.

To Nikki Giovanni for taking the time to write a letter to a "nobody" and for telling me, "to either say it or to go find something else to do!"

To Oprah and Maya Angelou for freeing the caged bird within me.

To the late, great Langston Hughes for asking, "What happens to a dream deferred?" in his poem, "Harlem."

ABOUT THE AUTHOR

Tammy Woodard Rivers has written 7 collections of poetry totaling over 500 poems. She has also written her autobiography that details her life of her struggle from child abuse. She attended Memphis State University and has been writing poems for over 15 years. Some of her poems have been sold in the gift shop of the Martin Luther King Jr. National Civil Rights Museum in Memphis, Tennessee.

A mother of three, she has struggled to overcome the devastating effect child abuse had on her. Moreover, she has successfully met the unrelenting challenges of breaking the cycle though acknowledgement of her past, prayer, counseling and the deep desire to give her children a better life than she had. More than anything she wishes to see her children find home to be the most loving and safest place in the world.

She has been married for 14 years to her second husband, who faced just as many challenges as she has by being married to a survivor of child abuse.

Table of Contents

Preface	11
PART ONE — A CHILD'S PAIN	13
The Kind Of House That ...	14
Home	16
We Grew Up	18
Expressions	18
Forever Scarred	19
Battered Child	20
No Name	21
Piercing Eyes	22
Wasn't Bout Me	22
Headphones	23
Split	24
Momma, Let Me Help You	25
Vicious Tongue	26
Don't Expect	27
Gone In An Instant	28
Whispers	29
All Along	29
PART TWO — PREADULTHOOD	31
Scarred Fruit	32
Rage	33
With Words At A Loss	34
Learned Your Lesson Well	35
Forget It	36
The Fear Of Living	36
The Past	37
He's In Control	38
Unglued	39
No One Knows	40
Moon After Moon	41
Created Clouds	42

Table of Contents

Easy	42
Grandma Said	43
My Potential	44
Won't Trust Myself	45
Someone To ...	46
The Unloved	47
To Be Beautiful	47
Giggle, Giggle, Giggle	48
Without Love	48
Odd Love From Father	49
Worthwhile	50
Were They Right?	51
That The World May Never See	52

PART THREE   ADULTHOOD   53

Acknowledging The Pain   53

Over And Done	54
Who Am I	55
Jesus, I'm Calling On You	56
Undeserved Debts	57
Do I Know?	58
Life's Edge	59
Enough	60
Repetition	61
I Mourn The Child	63
Pretty Wrappings	65
Wait On tomorrow	65
I'll Fall In Love With Me	66
Buried Pain	67
Hating Myself	68
I Freed Myself	69
Let Your Beauty Shine Through	71
You'll Live It Through	72
Back Burner	73
They Couldn't	74
Bitter	75

Table of Contents

PART THREE   ADULTHOOD   77

Rage   77

Should We Forget?	78
Who's Changed	79
True	80
I Feel	81
Manipulation	82
I Point My Finger At You	83
Absent	83
Perfect Picture	84
Why Mother?	85
All I See	86
The Past Is Not Your Enemy	87
Won't Pretend	88
WhoYou Really Are	88
Family	89
Severed	89
Target	90
Not For Sale	90
Admonished	91
Lies Of Love	92
Damage Done	92
Beast	93
I've Locked The Gate	93
My Feelings For You	94
Fate In The Supermarket	96
You Didn't Come	97
"Right" Is Right	98
Daddy's Payback	99

PART FOUR   ABUSED WOMAN   101

When That's All I Know	102
Lover	102
Loving	103
Do You Feel	105
My Pride	106

Table of Contents

They Wanted Blood	107
Cry Privately	108
Cause I	109
"High Yellow"	110
I'm Not Ashamed	111
Lines On Her Face	113
I've Seen The Other Side	115
Not Scared Anymore	116
One Day You'll See My Greatness	118
Haunted	120
And She's A Pretty Girl!	122
That Pretty Girl	124
I Didn't Cry	124
That Is Not My Brother	125
I Drank The Wine But...	126
... But I Never Thought He'd Rape Me	128
Reminding Mother	130
You Know the Molester	131
To The Rapist	132
That Woman Didn't Make You	134
Friend To The End	137

PART FIVE   MOTHERHOOD — 138

Suicide	139
Baby In Me	139
Body Of My Body, Soul Of My Soul	140
Deep Brown Eyes	142
Without Making A Sound	143
How Black Is You Heart?	144
I Am What I Am	145
It Could've Been Me	146
A Mother Cries	147
My Cruelty	147
To Jennie	148
That's My Dream	149
Nobody Had To Tell Me ...	150

Table of Contents

Soon As Daddy Is Home	153
Parents	154
PART SIX: SURVIVOR	**156**
The Battle Of My Life	157
Finally Me	158
To Touch The Rising Sun	159
On Me All Along	160
Someone Is My Name	162
My Name	163
So They Would Like Me	164
Good-bye	165
I Survived You	166
Through It All	167
I'm A Trooper	168
Now Just Look At Me	169
Blend In	171
Yet I Became	172
My Perspective	173
More Like You Than Not	174
Yet I Feel	175
Dear Daddy	176
Regrets	177
Just That She Lives	178
To Momma	179
Full Of Promise	180
In For The Count	181
I Outdid You, Pop!	182
I'll Speak	183
I Remember Heaven	184
The Father That I Love	185
The Perfect Father	186
Forget To Remember	187
I Am	188

"What Goes On In This House, Stays In This House!"

PREFACE

No one could possibly imagine the countless amount of hours that I've agonized over whether or not to publish this book. Writing the poems was not at all difficult.

They came naturally over time. They were my way of expressing so many of the things that I could not say. I've felt every emotion there is as I wrestled with the guilt from my decision to publish this book.

Of course "betrayal" for exposing myself and what I experienced at the hands of my parents and others were at the top of the list. I absolutely did not write this book to cause harm to anyone. I wrote this book to say what I needed to say and compiled these poems from several other collections of my poetry because I knew that they told the story of my deepest feelings more clearly than I could ever speak them.

For so many years, I've carried around so much pain, which I felt should be hidden out of respect and loyalty to my parents. But now I know that with all that is going on in the world and with all that I have experienced, this is a story which needs to be told. These emotions need to be expressed, no holds barred.

This book is about every child out there who is trying to say something that he/she cannot find the words to say or the courage with which to say them. This book is also about every parent out there that wonders what effect their abuse will have on their child. This book also is the answer to so many questions that our society is asking about how the world got to be in the shape that it is in.

May every person that reads this book make a positive change in his or her life and especially in the life of his or her child. May a child sleep peacefully and without fear because a parent heeded my words. May I become a better parent for writing this because "I'm not perfect."

"What Goes On In This House, Stays In This House!"

Part One

A Child's Pain

"What Goes On In This House, Stays In This House!"

The Kind Of House That...

It was the kind of house that
I used to drive by and wonder,
What kind of people lived inside?
Did they speak my language
And eat the bread that I ate?
Did they have the thoughts and wishes that I had?
Did they dream the dreams that I did?
Did they drink, argue and curse
Or raise their voices and get mad?
Did they worry my kind of worries
Or fight my kind of battles?
Were their scars buried deep within,
Just as mine were?
Did they sometimes cry alone,
Shout up to God
Or fall down to the ground?
Did they laugh so hard
That they -- OOPS! -- lost control?
Did they get down
And each night on their knees pray
To see a better day?
Did they ever stop and say, "Why me?",
"Why must I feel this way?"
Were there mornings that they wished hadn't come?
Were there nights that they hoped
To never see the sun?
Did they ever stop to watch a bird feed?
Did they ever take a look at the trees?
Did they sometimes rush so, through the day,
That they hardly even noticed
The sky, ground or flower?
Did they sometimes wish
To walk in the rain?
Did they get up to watch

Tammy Woodard Rivers

The soft falling snow?
Were there nights that they slept in the nude?
Were there nights that they slept
Not at all?
Did they ever stop
To wish upon a star
And wonder what was beyond the moon?
I do so wonder,
What the people are like
Who live in that house,
The kind my dreams
Are all about!

"What Goes On In This House, Stays In This House!"

HOME

*No one could see
That something was wrong.
All they could see was a happy home:
Toys galore everywhere,
A pretty rose house
With a gold painted stair,
A mom and dad always well dressed,
Three pretty children decked out in their best,
Always involved in The Homecoming scene,
Glittered down in every child's dream,
Freezer filled with food to the top
And a house so quiet
You could hear a pin drop.
Everything always in its place
People only saw contentment on their faces.
But no one ever bothered
To look any closer
Some even frowned and hated their good fortune.
If only they had once
Just looked past the film,
No doubt they would've seen the gloom,
An unsafe house that "was" no home,
A place that love had never known,
A dungeon where three frightened babes were sentenced,
The place the "evil" fire breathing dragon invented,
Doomed to a life of drudgery,*

Tammy Woodard Rivers

Trying their "best" to please misery,
A slap in the face
To keep the house clean,
A punch with a fist
Because the grass is green,
Told they were never good enough,
Forced to eat
Like a turkey you'd stuff,
Thanking thy father
For the fruit he bestowed,
Hoping to convince him
And not be punched in the nose,
That place where Mom was pushed around
And several times
Knocked to the ground.

"What Goes On In This House, Stays In This House!"

We Grew Up

*We grew up
with the police
Knocking at our door at night.
Afraid we were
When they fought
To try to help in their plight.
We buried our heads in pillows
To try to escape the scene
But what we felt was fear
Of growing up with our genes.*

EXPRESSIONS

My mother wasn't there
As I suffered each blow,
Never was there
For things I didn't know,
Always off to her own world
Searching for her space,
Never stopping to look at
The expression on my face.

Tammy Woodard Rivers

FOREVER SCARRED

Beautiful child born perfect
Cursed by thy own father's hand,
Handicapped in the mind
By fate's unwelcomed time.

Did your best, my child,
To be who "they" wanted you to be.
No normal child though
Could succeed, don't you see?

Yes, the blows you suffered
Were unjust from the start,
And unfortunately, my dear child,
They left you forever scarred.

For your illness there's no cure
That the doctor can prescribe,
And no one will ever see
All that you've been denied.

You feel alone and won't discuss
The pain that you suffer.
Day to day's normalities are like
A war without a buffer.

You continue in your stride,
Though you know there's no perfect answer.
What's over and done for some,
Is the beginning of your cancer!

"What Goes On In This House, Stays In This House!"

BATTERED CHILD

She just kept asking,
"Why did I pay the price, Lord?
Why did I have to?
Do we, as children,
Pay for what our parents have done?
I was only a child,
What did I do so wrong?
Why did I have to pay that price?
I don't believe
You wanted to punish me.
Why did I suffer?
Where was I wrong?
Should I pay for all
That my father has done?
Should we, as children, realize
That we must pay
For our fathers?"

Tammy Woodard Rivers

NO NAME

We lived in the same house,
Yet he had no name;
Not Dad, not Sir, not Pops or Father.
We saw each other everyday
And spoke as I'd go out to play.
"Good evening", I was taught to say.
Sometimes he'd grunt.
At other times ...not a sound
And he had no name,
Not "Hey you", not even "Uh",
Just, "Good Evening".
I guess maybe that "was" his name,
We were "of" the same blood we were told,
Yet he had no name.
No matter how hard I'd try
To force my mouth,
The word "Daddy" seemed to freeze
On my tongue.
And as for smiles, we had none.
I'd try hard to converse on special occasions
But my mind would come to a screeching halt.
I'd try and try but my thoughts were not.
I had none.
I had nothing to talk about because
He had no name.

"What Goes On In This House, Stays In This House!"

PIERCING EYES

Won't close my eyes right now
To see your piercing eyes,
All red and runny and scary
Piercingly staring at me.
You cry and whimper
Of how you love me so
And beat the Hell out of me
With the next breath.
Your stare says one thing
While your mouth says something else!

Wasn't Bout Me

**Wasn't bout me
What Daddy done.
Wasn't bout me at all.
Wasn't bout me
When he got the gun
And ran Momma down the hall.
Wasn't bout me at all,
Not at all.**

Tammy Woodard Rivers

HEADPHONES

A drunken father
Calls his daughter
To talk in the night.
Headphones, headphones--,
He's been listening to a song.
Bloodshot eyes peering,
As he speaks of S-E-X,
His needled five o'clock shadow
Scratches her tender skin.
He talks of boy do's and don'ts
As he piercingly draws her in.
He tells her that he loves her,
As his stare seeks control,
From eyes to crotch,
From eyes to crotch,
His eyes take her in.
The house is still and quiet.
No one's there
To lift his eyes from her face.
Fear grips her,
As she tries to hide
That she'd rather be another place.
No one to call,
No one to help
Or answer her silent cries.
Fear-- fear smothers her,
As she stares into his eyes.
Forever these sessions seem to last
To a child of eleven years old.
How can I explain to another
The secrets that I hold?

"What Goes On In This House, Stays In This House!"

SPLIT

I took myself away from there
A long time ago.
My spirit split and hid itself
From my own face.
I no longer "felt".
No longer did I exist.
What happened then
Was not to me,
So "feel", I did not do.
I felt no sympathy for me
Nor all of my "woe".
A stranger to myself,
How could I begin to feel?
"I", became "we"
Whenever I spoke to me.
Voices began to dance
Through conversations, three.
Arguments occurred,
Which always found replies.
There I watched the weak
Lose through every try.
Cruel names, I heard myself called.
Critical voices said,
"You're bad!,"
"You evil child!,"
"You will never succeed,"
"Though you may achieve."
"You shall never arrive,"
"Though you may learn to drive."
"For you are not good enough"
"To see beyond this door."
And for that reason,"
"You'll never reach your core."

Tammy Woodard Rivers

MOMMA, LET ME HELP YOU

Momma please, please don't cry.
I came here to help you.
I know that I am young
And haven't seen much world
But Momma I love you
And I know I want more for you.
So many nights,
I've heard him hit you
And in the morning
I've seen the pain
Along with the marks on your face.
Momma hold my hand,
I'll help you walk through the door.
You'll feel relief
When you're out on the street.
Please Momma, don't hang around
And let him sock you.
Momma I know you better than he does
And you don't deserve to be treated this way.
You're not those things he calls you.
I can see all of your good
And he no longer can.
I doubt if he ever could.
Come on Momma, I'll show you the way.
I know I'm still a child.
I know Daddy loves me
And I don't want to choose
Between you two,
But Momma I've watched silently
For far too long
And Momma I don't like
What's going on in our home.

"What Goes On In This House, Stays In This House!"

VICIOUS TONGUE

Say it to the child
And you say it to the adult
For the child becomes an adult
And carries what you say.

Your mean vicious tongue
Shall remain in the mind.
Any chance to reconcile
From that point on you forfeit

And though you failed to realize
The depth of your crime
From this point on
You pay a price.

The mind of a child
Shall never forget
While all of your viciousness
Becomes the child's.

All the pain and anger you've bestowed
Turns to hostility.
Hostility turns to brutality and revenge,
Though subconsciously it's conceived.

Rape, murder, hatred and greed
Came from your vicious seed.
"You're ugly, black and nothing."
"You won't never be nothing."

"You're stupid, dumb, crazy"
"Nobody wants you!"
"Who cares what you think."
"You're fat, skinny, funny looking."

"Your momma didn't want you."
"Your daddy neither."
"You don't even know who he is."
"You're just like him or her."

Say it and you'll pay
When you can't walk down the street
Nor sit on your front porch
Or worse yet, when you end up all alone.

Don't Expect

*Don't expect them
To do what is right, my child.
They have no concept
Of what is right,
Only of what feels good.*

"What Goes On In This House, Stays In This House!"

GONE IN AN INSTANT

He was far more intelligent
Than I.
He could see things
That I could not see,
Things that I would not see.
He felt the pain
From ten thousand years,
The pain of being gay,
The pain of saying nay.
Arrested, tried and convicted
From the very start,
Some said they saw gentility,
Others saw all heart.
Whatever it was,
Whatever he had
Was gone in an instant,
As they accused, slandered
And beat him.
He lost who he was,
Who he was to be,
Never to return,
As he witnessed around him
Destruction, brutality and inhumanity
All in a name,
"Mother".

Tammy Woodard Rivers

Whispers

Whispers saved me,
The whispers of a child,
Prayers made to God
From when I was young.
Whispers was my soul,
Crooned into my ear.
"You will succeed.
Just listen to what I have to say."
"Listen to the voice
Buried deep within.
Save yourself, my child,
I am on your side."
Be silent and you will hear
The whispers
That will save your life.

ALL ALONG

Someone all along,
But you would not see it.
Special deep inside,
But you would not seek it.
A message all along,
But you would not hear it.
Gifted all along,
But you wouldn't unwrap it,
Perfect all along.
But you couldn't accept it.
Your child all along,
But you didn't deserve it.

"What Goes On In This House, Stays In This House!"

Part Two

Preadulthood

"What Goes On In This House, Stays In This House!"

SCARRED FRUIT

Born the child,
Become adult,
Scars that never leave.
Wicked world,
Poisoned fruit
From an evil tree.
Change occur
We all ask
Of The Tree Of Life.
Ignore the child,
Forfeit the world,
The earth
And the flower.

Tammy Woodard Rivers

RAGE

He learned
From every lick and pop
How to keep quiet.
Smacked, kicked and knocked
And not a sound was uttered.
Stomped, choked and dragged
But still,
He wouldn't open his mouth
'Til he was grown
And frustration set in and
... Out Flew Rage
All covered in blood.

"What Goes On In This House, Stays In This House!"

WITH WORDS AT A LOSS

They wouldn't listen
When I was a child.
So it's hard to believe
That I'm of value now.
As I struggle to get my point across,
I'm suddenly with words at a loss.
For when does justice finally occur
For brutality deemed obscure?
As I scrub my face
And grit my teeth,
I wonder what will become of me.
For such a crime
A stranger would be punished.
Yet I'm the one
Left defending myself.
As I tell my tales of my plight from thunder,
I find my name being admonished.
To save my name,
Pretend nothing happened.
As I listen to stories
Of devotion and love,
I become so filled
With rage and disgust,
I'm suddenly overcome by my unjust.

Tammy Woodard Rivers

LEARNED YOUR LESSON WELL

Danger is in the air.
You know more than the teacher.
From him, you gained your start.
Through you he found his heart.

"Now you dare to surpass me!
Belittling all that I could not be?"
The student becomes the teacher.

Fire and rain
Disguised as pain
Run rampart through my heart,
Then suddenly, I'm forever scarred.

You proved to me
All I could not see,
Showed to me
What I'll never be.

You teacher of the teacher,
You learned your lesson well
But failed to become,
My pride.

"What Goes On In This House, Stays In This House!"

FORGET IT?

Leave it behind
And forget,
I know you wish to say.
You'll be the first
He'll meet on judgment Day.

THE FEAR OF LIVING

Too scared to live
Too afraid to die
Too scared to even
Reach up to the sky

Tammy Woodard Rivers

THE PAST

I will not close my eyes,
Will not let it die.
It lives inside my soul.
It's a part of who I am.
Time will not erase it,
Won't even shrink it.
That part of me
Will always be,
Even when I'm gone.
There's no fight to win,
Nothing to gain,
Except me.

"What Goes On In This House, Stays In This House!"

HE'S IN CONTROL

I look out of the window
And then he appears,
A piece from yesterday.
He smiles at me,
For he knows
For now, he's in control.
We go up hills and mountains,
That I don't wish to see;
While running down I feel feelings,
I've never wished to feel.
He speaks in his same voice
That I so obviously remember.
I am meek, silent and frail,
Just as I was back then.
I am the virgin
And he is my teacher,
As I obey his calls.
Then suddenly I awake,
Shivering, wet and cold.
I am scared, angry and confused.
Why did I dream that dream?
He laughs,
For only he knows
The answer.

Tammy Woodard Rivers

UNGLUED

What could possibly be worst
Than waking from a nightmare?
How about not knowing
What you're waking from?
Your pulse is faster,
Your breathing sporadic
And you're shaking from head to toe
But for the life of you,
You can't begin to explain.
You lost that thought,
Whatever it was.
You can't set it straight.
There's no way possible,
With no where to start.
You tell yourself, "Don't worry about it.
It was just a dream."
You haven't a single justification
For why you've become unglued.
Getting through the day,
It seems over and done
But deep in the mind
Is a victory never to be won.
You conclude that you have a weakness
But can't understand what it is.
Astronaut, president or chimney sweeper,
Those labels are all useless
When dealing with what you feel.

"What Goes On In This House, Stays In This House!"

NO ONE KNOWS

No one knows the darkness
Of our deepest, darkest hour.
No one knows our sadness.
No one knows our pain.

No one knows our hopes,
Or all of our fears.
No one knows what truly
Drives us all to tears.

We walk sometimes a lonely road
That others somehow partake;
A man alone in a jungle,
Surviving for survival's sake.

We claw, scratch, bite and destroy
The barriers in our way.
We know that someday, somehow
We'll make it out to play.

We'll silently sit in the sun
As the seagulls fly our way,
And find the strength within our hearts
To say good-bye to yesterday.

Tammy Woodard Rivers

MOON AFTER MOON

He enters my dreams.
He harasses my being.
He forces me to remember his reign
While burning my soul
And destroying my mind.
He won't leave me along.
When did the nightmare start?
Where will I go from here?
Madness is the only answer for me.
I want him to leave me along,
To go away forever
But he visits me time and time again.
I have no choice but to let him in.
What can I do?
What can I say?
Who can help my dreams?
I don't believe I put him there.
Why would I want to feel fear
Night after night,
Moon after moon?
I try not to sleep;
That way, I'm in control.
My eyes are black.
My face is worn.
My skin is gray.
What's gonna happen to me,
Now?

"What Goes On In This House, Stays In This House!"

CREATED CLOUDS

I CREATE THE CLOUDS IN MY LIFE.
I CREATE THE TEARS,
PURPLE, RED AND BURNT ORANGE CLOUDS
THAT COMPLICATE MY LIFE.
I LOVE THE CLOUDS
FOR THEY ARE MY SALVATION.
THEY ARE MY MONDAY
MORNING BLUES.
I REACH OUT AND TOUCH
SPECKS OF MY UNFULFILLMENT.

EASY

Easier to blame me
Than to accept what's going on.
Easier to say I'm wrong
Than to say it's you.
Must blame myself
And say I'm no good
Rather than to lose
Something I know I should.
Don't want to accept
That you're not there.
Easier to see,
I'm wrong,
No Matter where.

Tammy Woodard Rivers

GRANDMA SAID

*Just shut your mouth
And suffer it through.
No one here
Gives a damned about you,
So what, you were here
When I needed you.
Life doesn't begin
Or end with you.
Got my own worries,
My own problems.
Just keep it to yourself
And bare it.
No big deal
That you feel pain,
Right now from you,
I have nothing to gain.
Leave me alone
And go away.
That's all I've got to say.*

"What Goes On In This House, Stays In This House!"

MY POTENTIAL

*Scared to take a chance,
Too much to lose,
Afraid to walk in
Someone else's shoes.
The good and bad,
I know about.
Can't take a chance.
Might end up living
Worst than I am.
Know what I've got.
Know where I am.
Easier to accept.
The things I am not.
To take a chance
Confuses me
About who I am.
Better to accept me
Now as I stand
I'm not a winner
Not a failure,
Nothing today.
Easier to keep me
Just as I'll stay.*

Tammy Woodard Rivers

WON'T TRUST MYSELF

Just listen to myself,
I know the perfect answer.
It's hidden beneath the surface,
Afraid to stand out.
I search here and there
For someone to show me out.

Buried deep inside,
It shouts to get out.
I push it in harder.
Can't trust what it must say.
If I listen to myself
And I am found wrong,
I'll never trust me again,

So I have to be strong.
Won't listen to myself.
Can't listen to myself.
Don't want to be wrong.
I'd rather trust another.
They know where I belong.
Insecurity, that's me.

"What Goes On In This House, Stays In This House!"

SOMEONE TO ...

I always searched outside
For what I could not find,
Someone to love and hear me,
Someone to think tenderly of me.

A soft voice and gentle face,
I always believed was good.
But isn't a war
Often won quietly?

Looking for the right thing
In the wrong person,
How could I even know
What I was searching for?

Who could I trust?
Who can I now trust?
Certainly not you, not even me.
I am not safe.

The Unloved

The spirit dies
When love is continuously denied
As the fumes of desperation
Exaggerates and slowly shows its face
On the unloved
For whom only death
Can give love a second chance.

TO BE BEAUTIFUL

I've got everything in my bathroom
To make me beautiful
But I don't care about beauty.
Something in me is dead,
Stone cold dead
And so is my fire,
Along with the flame,
Extinguished by fingertips.
A long time ago
I died.

"What Goes On In This House, Stays In This House!"

Giggle, Giggle, Giggle

Giggle, giggle, giggle,
I used to be called.
If only they could see me now,
That I hardly ever smile.

My giggles weren't about being happy.
They were about my not believing
in who I was,
Being afraid and not knowing
How to express myself.

WITHOUT LOVE

I'll never share a football game
Or cotton candy at the fair.
Nor can I tell you all about
Happy times never there.

What I have to say
You don't wish to hear.
It's unsavory and distasteful
Without love and good cheer.

As I listen to your joys about yesterday,
I sit quietly cause all I can remember
Are bad and sad memories
That I've put away.

Tammy Woodard Rivers

Odd Love From Father

True love
Is strange to me,
Like a foreign country.
I can't comprehend
What is being said.

I don't know how to answer.
I never learned the language.
I find it odd and disgusting
When I try to take it in;

A father loving a daughter
With tender gentle hands,
A father hugging a wife
with love in his heart.

I know mother love
Of which I'm unsure.
A kind and gentle father
Is something I never had.

"What Goes On In This House, Stays In This House!"

WORTHWHILE

People running
 In and out of your life,
You wonder why they go.
Why won't they stay?

If you can always rememberThe time you had together
 And if you look deep inside,
You'll find it all worthwhile.

Even though they left,
 Whichever way,
Stop and think of all the things
That they left you with.

Whether good or bad,
 The memories do count.
You learned, grew and gained from them,
Though you can't see it clearly.

If you'll just be strong,
 You'll eventually realize
That you're a far greater person
Because of them.

Because of something they said,
 Because of what they did,
And because of who they were,
You're a deeper Being.
You're a brighter star.

For everything there is a reason,
 Though the pieces aren't together.
Your life was enriched by everything you touched.
Just take the time to look all around.

Tammy Woodard Rivers

WERE THEY RIGHT ?

Why could others see in me
Greatness, that I could not see?
Why could they feel the fire
That I could not feel?

They said I had potential
A long time ago,
Said I'd one day reach a height,
That I deserved it all.

Were they prophets
That could see the light
Or did I fool them
Like I'm something that I am not?

Am I just a common man?
Maybe but maybe not.
Called by name to greatness,
Said I'd make a change.

Let them be right
And prove to me I'm wrong,
For I never saw the greatness,
Just that I was strong.

"What Goes On In This House, Stays In This House!"

THAT THE WORLD MAY NEVER SEE

No one knows what lies within the spirit,
What flies within the heart,
To every man there are complexities
That the world may never see.
We wear a mask
That to the shallow
Sums up our worth,
But buried deep inside of us all
Is a whole other life.
We choose to whom and when
We'll shed a touch of light,
And when we do,
More often than not,
We reveal a brighter day,
We show another way.
To sum me up by only
Looking at my face,
Sums you up because
You've simply lost the race,
The Human Race!

Part Three

Adulthood

Acknowledging The Pain

"What Goes On In This House, Stays In This House!"

OVER AND DONE

You want to let go of your past
But you see faces and places
And feelings as clear as the morning sun.
You wonder why the thoughts occur.
Am I a weaker man
For holding on to what's over and done,
Things I can never change?
I am wise and don't like the pain;
So why must I visit that place again?
Everything is as it was,
Nothing ever changes.
I am different
But can I be the same,
To dream a dream,
To have a thought
Or do I just like pain?
Am I different from others?
Do they dream the same,
Of a past that's gone
So many yesterdays ago?
Does it all remain?
Am I a lesser man?

Tammy Woodard Rivers

WHO AM I

Little voice
Stop talking to me.
Little girl
Set me free.
When will I be
Who I am?
When will you
Leave me along?
I know you
From the past
But please,
Can't we part company
Little girl
That I see
In me.

"What Goes On In This House, Stays In This House!"

JESUS I'M CALLING ON YOU

I have a hole embedded
Deep down in my heart.
Only one can help me.
Only one can save me.
Jesus, I'm calling on you
To mend my damaged soul.
Give me love, strength and knowledge.
Show me how to love.
I'm crying everyday,
Though sometimes even I don't know.
I'm broken into hundreds of pieces
And can't solve the puzzle,
So Jesus I'm calling on you
To give me a strategy.
Where does the first piece fit?
Where should I start?
Help me Jesus.
Help me mend my broken heart.

Tammy Woodard Rivers

UNDESERVED DEBTS

So unfair
To be born wronged,
Through life you stumble,
Through love you bumble.
You wonder why
You owe the debt.
Is it from your past?
Does your past begin?
Before life is conceived?
If so then
Is your debt
Ever paid
For things never purchased?

"What Goes On In This House, Stays In This House!"

DO I KNOW?

How much do I know
That I don't know?
Probably all of it I'm sure,
But so much is locked away
In a safe of mine,
And right now
I don't know that old combination.
I guess I'll have to
Get a locksmith
To break open the lock,
And after I do
Maybe I'll tell you
Just how much I know.

LIFE'S EDGE

Flirt with death
You sweet, sweet child
From a broken home.
Difference unknown
To everyone
Who walks in your path.
Lived a life
Of abuse and misuse
In every way,
Everyday.
So why not you figure,
Just end it all this way.
A life so unfair,
To you it seems it's aimed
To feel all of life's
Unforgivable pain.

"What Goes On In This House, Stays In This House!"

ENOUGH

My child,
I'm sorry to see you suffer,
Suffer through your life,
Sad to see you ponder
And seldom choose what's right.
You don't understand why fate
So often throws you ditches.
I know of the pain
You suffer from day to day.
I want to reach out
And touch your sweet hand
And help you out again,
But this time, dear brother,
I'm afraid you'll pull me in,
So I shy away from you.
I no longer know what to say
And struggle with simplicity.
"How are you?"
"What's going on?"
"Did you notice the weather?"
"I'll talk to you later, brother."

Tammy Woodard Rivers

REPETITION

I find myself wishing
To make the same mistake,
Even though I know for me,
It only holds heartache.

Force myself to suffer hurt
And pain I seem to hunger.
I guess I feel that I deserve
A painful life of blunder.

My past screams to be renewed
And brought into today.
Heartache, hurt and pain
Is the only comfortable way.

God, what a sad existence,
That only I seem to know.
I don't want peace, quiet or tranquillity,
Just to be dealt another blow.

To ride that stretch of rode "Danger",
I wish to live on the edge,
To scream, kick and fight
Before I am dead.

Peace for me bores me to death
And cheats me of myself.
Passion good or bad,
Lets me feel I took a breath.

"What Goes On In This House, Stays In This House!"

I'll flirt with death
With no regrets
And if it catches me,
I'll gladly relinquish myself.

In some mysterious way,
Until I reach the edge,
I'll never feel totally full,
Like I'm out on a ledge.

Tammy Woodard Rivers

I MOURN THE CHILD

I mourn the child that I have lost
Forever deep inside of me,
Promises I made, I'll never keep
Buried deep inside of me.

I cry at night
For the babe crying out yet silently.
Thought in time I'd comfort me.
Thought I'd be all I wanted to be.

My life is over, lost forever
Deep inside a dream.
I died years ago, though I somehow survived
In a brand new me.

Disappointed, my head hangs low
For the child crying inside of me.
How can I comfort, hold and love her,
That little apple-eyed child?

I do love her so
But just can't seem to help her.
She's so timid, sad and hurt.
She's full of anger, rage and hate.

Yet still she's full of love.
How do I comfort the child inside my heart
Crying out for me always
To never slip and fall?

"What Goes On In This House, Stays In This House!"

She never allows mistakes, that part of me, the child.
She follows me wherever I go
And reminds me of our pain.
She never forgives the rain.

She sways in like the wind
And swoops down like a storm.
In the end, she leaves me wondering
Just what did I do wrong.

She refuses to leave my side
And always holds my hand.
How can I deny her my love when everyone else did?
Won't share her, only tell you what she says is ok.

Pretty Wrappings

I keep wondering
What is missing,
What I'm searching for.
I believed I would find it
In a pearly jar,
Believed that pretty wrappings
Was the true answer.
Found that no matter what,
I'll never get it back.

WAIT ON TOMORROW

I'm gonna pull myself together
And be who I am.
What you see is suffering.
It's not really me.

From deep inside my heart,
The pain seems so severe.
Preoccupied with the pain
Is my shame.

But one day the pain is gonna stop.
I'll just wait until tomorrow
And then I'll get better.
Just you wait and see.

"What Goes On In This House, Stays In This House!"

I'LL FALL IN LOVE WITH ME

I remember the love
I used to have for me.
One day it will return.
I know it will,
After the pain goes away.
I'll remember me
And I'll love me more
Than I ever did before.
I'll fall in love
All over again
Like a child does
With his mother,
With me, nobody but me.
I'm gonna be a better lover
To me than I've ever been.
One of these days
I'm gonna love me again,
Any one of these old days.

Tammy Woodard Rivers

BURIED PAIN

I'm holding a lot in.
I can't get it out.
No matter how much I try.
I just don't know how deep it is.

I don't know where it is.
I just can't reach the pain.
I so much want to.
I want to explain it to you.

But I just can't reach in
And pull it out.
It's so deep.
Buried so deep.

It just leaves me drained
Every time I reach in.
So baby, here is my love.
Here is my love.
Please don' hurt it.

Cause I'll never reach it again if you do.
I want to open up
But so many times before when I did,
You wouldn't understand, you wouldn't let me in.

I won't take the chance again
But burying it hurts so.
The pain is so severe
It just leaves me afraid.

How can I open up
And tell you how I really feel?
How can I let you play around
With my soul again?

"What Goes On In This House, Stays In This House!"

HATING MYSELF

Just when did I learn to hate myself?
Was it a long time ago?
For what reason or purpose
Did hating myself serve?

Was the feat accomplished,
That which was so heavily bestowed on me?
Mission accomplished finally!
Is that what you say?

A learned pattern of life
That I'm hating to live.
Wish I could be a star
But even if I were a star

Shining brightly in the sky,
I wonder could I still find
Reason to hate who I am.
It would even be better to hate "what" I am

But to hate who I am,
Somebody told me to!
I never should have listened
Because they just hated who they were to say that to me.

I Freed Myself

Didn't want to admit
That I hated me.
Couldn't understand
Who I could not be.

Wondering why most others
Were so unlike me,
"Do you hate yourself sometimes?",
I'd ask of thee.

Such far-fetched a question
To which they couldn't relate,
"Hate myself?"
"Never dear!" is what they would say.

What's normal for me
Sadly was off the wall for most.
Took years for me to realize
That I hated you.

Wondering why so many times
I wasn't good enough,
Hating you finally freed me
To finally love myself.

"What Goes On In This House, Stays In This House!"

Thought I must be bad
To hate my own father.
No matter what you'd done,
"Daddy, I've got to be wrong."

Why else would you hurt me
Refuse to love me,
And always find my wrong,
One so big and strong?

Tammy Woodard Rivers

LET YOUR BEAUTY SHINE THROUGH

You don't have to be
What they want you to be.
You don't have to die to be you.
You are free.
You can be free,
Just look to your soul.
Look deep within
And let your beauty shine through.
The sadness that you feel
Is not because of you.
It's not your fault
That they can't see you,
A significant and unique spirit
In a big cold world.
I'm here to tell you
That I love you for who you are.
I don't want you to change.
Stay who you are
And please, don't think of dying.
This world needs you.

"What Goes On In This House, Stays In This House!"

YOU'LL LIVE IT THROUGH

Don't be afraid.
You'll survive it.
You'll live,
No matter what becomes of you,
You'll live it through.
They can beat you,
Cut off you head,
Or toss you to the lions
But you'll still live.
You'll live it through.
We were put on this earth
To live and to die
And all the in between,
Is for what you must strive,
To love, give and teach by living
To all that you can reach.
So close your eyes
And open them again
But this time
Refuse to let fear in

Tammy Woodard Rivers

Back Burner

Maybe I never realized
That I had been on my own already.
All the times I trusted in you
And you let me down,
I was alone,
As I picked myself up,
Polished myself off
And gleamed and glittered in the distance,
Lighting the way
And brightening a path
For someone else,
Always making a way
For those whom I trusted that were in need,
Always that perfect deed shone on my face,
Full speed ahead, charge,
For all in distress,
Never once stopping to see
That I deserved a rest,
Never once stopping for me to adjust and refuel,
Putting myself on the back burner
And eventually I forgot,
That the most important meal
Was cooking in "that" pot,
In someone else's pot.

"What Goes On In This House, Stays In This House!"

THEY COULDN'T

People always want you to be
What they could never be.
Kind, considerate, thoughtful and courteous
Is what they wish to see.

Asking more of you
Than they could do themselves.
"Kiss up, put up, and walk away."
Is all they seem to say.

Such demands they put on me
So I can be their fantasy.
Judging me when I choose to fight.
Discouraging me if I should bite.

I'll protect my own hand,
Something they could never do.
I know they will never understand
That fighting back gains respect too.

BITTER

The time has come,
Finally come that I should know the truth.
The friends I loved,
The love I loved
Was anything but true.
That invisible bond
That shone from me to you,
I must finally face
Didn't have a clue.
No, you were never mine.
You were never there.
What I conceived was love
Has left me pained and bare.
How could I see something
That never was to be?
How could I know
That I'd be left in such despair?
How much I loved thee once
When you were all mine.
Now I'm left with sadness
Whenever I look behind.
Sorrow envelops me
For the love I had for you.
I never knew my downfall
Would be to still love you.

"What Goes On In This House, Stays In This House!"

Part Three

Adulthood

Rage

"What Goes On In This House, Stays In This House!"

SHOULD WE FORGET?

Should we forget the good times
Because yesterday's gone?
Should the child forget the mother
That died yesterday?
Should I embrace the lion
That devoured my arm yesterday?
If I spat in you face yesterday,
Will you forget it today?
Well yesterday is today.
Will yesterday's rain
Not effect the farmer's crop today?
Will God forget yesterday
And send us all to Heaven?
Does who I was yesterday
Have no bearing on who I am today?
So don't you dare expect me
To forget about yesterday!

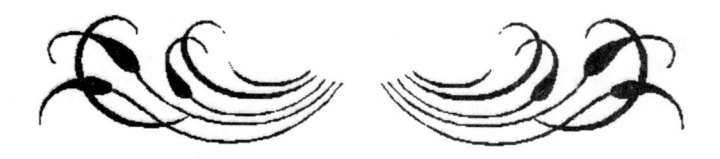

Tammy Woodard Rivers

Who's Changed

You say that you've changed.
Should I forget my scars?
Should I forget the pain?
What about me?
What about my name?
Just because you've changed your name,
Doesn't mean a thing.
Mine stayed the same.
I'm still the same heart.
I remember my yesterday.
Do you honestly believe
I could erase the memory from my mind,
Or from my soul?
Change all you want to
And fool those around you.
I know you deep within.
Yes, I know the person there,
Who he was yesterday
And will remain
Etched in my mind
Until the day I
Die!

"What Goes On In This House, Stays In This House!"

TRUE

"Sweet old man"
They say
About one so wrong.
"Evil old man"
I say
Of a soul gone astray.
Ruined me,
Ripped my soul in two
"Sweet old man".
You claim that you are true.
True of what; I must ask,
True of fresh new life,
True of a brand new heart and soul,
True of gentleness?
Fool the rest
But never me.
I know when I look at you
Just what I see,
The same mind,
The same heart and soul,
Wicked and old,
Scared
And running out of time,
"Sweet old man."

Tammy Woodard Rivers

I Feel

*No use in my pretending
That it's no big deal;
Fury is what I actually feel.
No pretending that I'm more than I am.
I'm just a simple man,
No Jesus Christ.
No one's always right.
I have feelings
That could possibly cut you like a knife.
I'm not sorry
For the feelings that I have,
Not sorry for seeming bad.
No pretension for pity's sake,
No trying to prove
That I'm a better man.
I'm frustrated and angry,
And I won't forgive,
Not this time!*

"What Goes On In This House, Stays In This House!"

MANIPULATION

Gentle kind voice
Smothering in nature
Disguised by concern
And pretentious mothering
Controlling little suggestions
Never directly conveyed

Eventually causing yourself
To be hated and despised
Determined never to release
The chain that you hide
In it breathes your life
Where you soar through the skies

You own another life
Of the one you say you love
Controlling mine and never having
To take control of yours.

Tammy Woodard Rivers

I POINT MY FINGER AT YOU

Though you never delivered a blow,
You perpetuated the violence
Through your silence.
Though you never actually stole
The sweet candy that you tasted,
You knew in your heart
From where it came.

ABSENT

You were there all along
But could not see the scene.
You closed your eyes and your ears
To deal with life so mean
And now to speak of the past
It's like you were not there.
A stranger could better understand
What you will not dare!

"What Goes On In This House, Stays In This House!"

Perfect Picture

You are blind!
Your whole life
You walked around
Seeing only what you wanted to see.

You're brilliant
To live in a world you choose
While life around you
Destroys those whom you should shield.

Life smashes that perfect picture,
Which on your bureau sits
As you wonder to yourself
What happened to love in it.

That which was never there,
Never can be born.
You saw a garden of flowers
Always in perfect bloom,

A perfect little family
In a perfect home.
How can I fulfill your fantasy
That I cannot comprehend?

I see disaster surrounding me.
I feel it in my heart
With eyes opened wide,
With data stored in my mind.

I saw what happened and every detail
Though you claim that you didn't
And now it's part of who I am.
Now it's my name.

Tammy Woodard Rivers

WHY MOTHER?

The core of the illness
I've finally found
Through cover-ups and turns around.
The answer lies within.
Every time I catch my breath
And start all over again,
"Mother, Mother" my insides keep saying,
"You let him beat, Humiliate and kill us
From the start."
And my question to you, dear Mother is,
"Where was your heart?"
We came from you, through you.
We breathed your breath of life
But when it came down to it,
To you, just what was right?
To hear your babes cry at night
And always in a shudder,
Was he worth the wrong,
My sweet and silent Mother?
You justified and denied
The wrong that surrounded you.
For every lick and pop,
I hold you responsible too.
Mother we are "of" you.
We are from you
But once our life began,
That was when you let it end.
Do you like what you see now,
Mother?

"What Goes On In This House, Stays In This House!"

All I See

Never were
What I thought you to be.
Never were
All that I see.
Couldn't believe
That you're not there.
Couldn't accept
That you don't care.
The more I tried
To delude myself,
The more I lied
And fooled myself.
The ones you love
Can hurt more than life.
The ones you love
Can cut like a knife.
No better,
No worse
Than anyone else,
The ones you love
Think only of themselves.

Tammy Woodard Rivers

The Past is Not Your Enemy

To escape our past
Is all we want to do
But how can we make go away
The only thing that's you?

We drink the wine of forgetfulness
To make it go away.
If only we could realize,
It just makes it stay.

Why don't we face it,
So the running will end?
It's time to stop and realize
The past is not your enemy; but your friend.

"What Goes On In This House, Stays In This House!"

WON'T PRETEND

Oh yes, I'm angry with you.
I'm disgusted by the things that you do.
I feel like such a fool
Because I opened up and believed in you.
I gave you a piece of me
For far too long.
I've been pushed around
For too long.
I've let you put me down
And I won't pretend any longer
That everything's okay.
I'm disappointed,
Even though I didn't have expectations.
I'm scared to death
Of the phony you are.

WHO YOU REALLY ARE

Don't worry about
Pretending with me.
Be yourself
And show me who you really are.
Run, run to the others.
Be at their beck and call.
Don't worry about me.
Don't even give me a thought.
Just be yourself
And I'll know just who you really are
And how much I mean to you.

Tammy Woodard Rivers

FAMILY

Insane Insanity,
That's what it is,
Family.
Ashamed, Humiliated and Disgraced,
Family
Disgust, Illusion and Manipulation,
Yet so much pride.
Pride?
Insane pride,
That it most definitely is,
Insanity.

SEVERED

I'm not gonna call apologizing,
Not this time my dear
Even if I was wrong,
I just can't do it any more.

I love you my sweet darling
And I'm sorry it ends this way
But the ties must be broken
And this is my only way.

There's no way to avoid hurting you
But this time I've got to think of me.
Good bye my sweet darling.
Maybe I'm wrong
But I've got to try this time to be strong.

"What Goes On In This House, Stays In This House!"

TARGET

I will no longer be
Your convenient little scapegoat,
Chewing a little sin today
And indignation tomorrow,
Blamed for the color of the sky
And man's essential breath,
Swallowing down the path of
The destiny that you've wroth.
Choking and finally vomiting up
All of your denial
Then looking into the mirror
And seeing the target of your frustration
Is me,
Innocent me.

NOT FOR SALE

I won't let you control me,
No matter what game you play.
I know the tricks.
I made up the game.
Forget it if you think
You've got me in your hand.
I'm willing to give up everything I have
To never be controlled by a foolish game.
I won't play by the rules
For the sake of your silly name.
You'll never be able to buy
Untouchable me.
I'm my own.
I belong to only me.

Tammy Woodard Rivers

ADMONISHED

As I scrub my face
And grit my teeth,
I wonder what will become of me.
For such a crime
A stranger would be punished,
Yet I'm the one defending myself
As I tell my tales
Of my plight from thunder,
I find my name
Being admonished.
To save my name,
Pretend nothing happened.
As I listen to stories
Of love and devotion,
I become filled
With rage and disgust.
I'm overcame by my unjust.
My father beat me.
My mother stood and watched.
I have no problem
With those that I know,
As long as I get some decency,
A word that means
So simple a thing.
When is it my turn to get some?

"What Goes On In This House, Stays In This House!"

LIES OF LOVE

You expect me to pretend
Like I really care.
You expect feelings.
That were never there.
I'm sorry.
That's asking
Too much of me.
I can only be
What I'm willing to be;
A liar, I am not.
Won't do the deed
Even if this time
Has a greater need.

DAMAGE DONE

The beast claimed
It's over and done

Claimed he's changed.
Forget the damage done
To those left behind.
New beast
Taught so well
Not to tell.

Tammy Woodard Rivers

BEAST

I guess the beast
Finally won out
And gobbled down your soul.
Now you are he
and he is you
and all that's left
of what you were,
Is what you used to be.

I'VE LOCKED THE GATE

Your love
Came a wee bit late.
My heart has now mended itself.
I've locked the gate
And refuse to tell you the password;
Refuse to give you a key.
When the door was open to love
You called it surrender.
When I offered to help you
You never tried to remember.
Now I refuse to let down my guard.
Though some days I am kind,
Most days I am outraged.
How can love
Get to where it is today?
Were the feeling I once had,
Real yesterday?
Where shall I go from here?
And as for you,
I don't care!

"What Goes On In This House, Stays In This House!"

My Feelings for You

Papa, no need to worry.
My feelings for you remain the same.
You are deeply rooted and embedded in
The depth of my memory.
Your outrage and unpredictable cruelty will always comfort me
Whenever I'm feeling happy, sad, insecure or scared.
The thoughts of you will never go away
And don't worry, you will always remain the same virile
And volcanic untouchable that you were then to me.
I'll never see a frail and broken man,
Only a beast that's out of control
That the devil himself created and sent
With no capacity to feel compassion, pain or sorrow
And I will in my mind remain a victim,
A very minute part of your existence
With feelings that no one on the planet deserves.
I will feel unwanted, unloved, undeserving
And unable to give all I wish to give.
Nothing I ever do will feel good enough
And instead of failing Algebra,
I'll fail at life, wake up in the morning,
Look myself in the mirror, not like who I see
And want help but fear reaching out to people
Who could possibly love me.
I'll always feel inferior to others,
Never quite human.
I'll stick my hand in to do or to give just a little bit
And always expect that hand to come back to me burned
Or beaten and it probably will for some unconscionable thing
That I've done, maybe needing, wanting or expecting too much.
I'll then return to that corner of my mind
Where you so often sent me, where I would rock my tattered,
Tear soaked broken little body to sleep,
Afraid to wake up and face another day,
Wondering why God won't take me home.
People always wonder if there really is a Heaven and a Hell,
Yet for me, I have no doubt,
For I've already seen Hell and I've lived with the devil.

Tammy Woodard Rivers

He exist in the man that I call daddy
And life for me, he made hell.
Oh, he never lets me live my life.
He always visits me late at night.
He wants me to remember his reign, his power,
Oh not a particular incident, he creates new unthinkable
Acts of horror and makes me remember my face, my outrage
And my hopelessness.
He may not only torture me as a child,
I see myself older, yet still I'm able to be violated
By this demonic creature.
Just when things start going right,
He tells me I'm no good, that I don't deserve life itself
Or anything in this life.
At one time when I was younger and stronger,
I would try to fight back
But years have passed and I've begun to wonder
If maybe I did something to deserve my pain.
Maybe I'm not liked by people because of who you said I am.
Maybe I'll never find peace or happiness
Because they see you in me,
Because I see you in me.
I can't make you disappear.
Guilt consumes me sometimes,
As I wonder if possibly my daddy loved me
But was out of control.
When I see him love other people,
I wonder why I never got that same love.
When I need someone to talk to,
I wonder why I feel so empty and so all alone.
I wonder why I never trust anyone around me.
I feel in my heart that they don't really care
And will one day walk out and leave.
Thank you so much Daddy for doing such a wonderful job,
The best you could do, I'm sure.

"What Goes On In This House, Stays In This House!"

FATE IN THE SUPERMARKET

We all stood there watching
Afraid to make a scene
But anger we all felt
To watch her destroy her gene.

How could she beat and humiliate
One such as her own?
As we watched we grew angrier at the fate
The child should never have known.

I'm sure it must have occurred to us all
What terrible things happen at home
For to beat her child and make him fall,
We knew she was worst than wrong.

At least eight of us saw
Her accusation of embarrassment
But we all knew of the law
That for this, time is spent
Not by the mother but by the child.

Are we all as guilty as she
For not helping that child?
Maybe possibly we could have helped
By stopping to talk for a while.

Tammy Woodard Rivers

YOU DIDN'T COME

Where were you
When I couldn't even breath from the pain?
Why didn't you call
When you saw the rain?
You say that you care
But can never be there.
What kind of love do you feel?
I ran through the storm
Screaming out your name.
I fell to the ground
Dying from the pain
But you didn't come.
Where were you, I want to know,
When the blood from my vein
Went spewing below?
Where were you then
I'd really like to know?
Why couldn't you be reached
When the darkness came?
Why weren't you around
Whenever I'd feel pain?
You say you love me
But left me all alone.
You say you care
But just couldn't be there,
Wouldn't be there.
I want to know
Where were you
When I needed you so?
Please, I've got to know.

"What Goes On In This House, Stays In This House!"

"RIGHT" IS RIGHT

I used to think that "Right" was right
And everybody knew.
Now I'm not so sure anymore.
So what's a person to do?

Go on living
In a world where dreams
Are supposed to come true
Or give it up and stay in
What appeals to you.

Arguing on absolute fact
Will not give justice its due.
Fighting for a crack to form
In such an imperfect stone.

People are our only hope
To save society.
What's right must matter then
To save the lives of man.

It's all a matter of perception
Some men will say.
It's the matter of deception
That's leading us all astray!

Tammy Woodard Rivers

DADDY'S PAYBACK

The child said to the mother,
"Why don't we pay back Daddy
For all the dirt he's done,
Now that he's sick and no longer strong.
Let's pay him back
For all the times I watched helplessly
As he beat you, Mother.
Let's show him how it feels
To be beaten by, another."
The mother turned around and said,
"My child, why should I beat a man
And condemn myself to Hell?
I don't wish to be what he was,
Now that he's half dead.
The price he pays everyday
Is worst than being dead.
It's Hell you know
Needing those you've hurt
To take care of you.
We remember every deed,
So he must remember too
And Hell is where he lives
Because everyone gets their due."

"What Goes On In This House, Stays In This House!"

Part Four

Abused Woman

"What Goes On In This House, Stays In This House!"

WHEN THAT'S ALL I KNOW

"Leave him
If
He ever hits you!"
You said on my wedding day.
"One time
Is all it takes,
You've got to make him pay!"
But Daddy dear,
How can I leave
When that's all I know?
Each time that "you" hit me,
Didn't I let it go?

LOVER

More vicious than any other,
Yet closer than even a mother,
Whose cruelty will not be disguised,
Not even by thine own eyes.

Tammy Woodard Rivers

LOVING

Hangover
Quiet comes
Memories
Saturday night
Accusations
Screaming
Insults
Humiliation
Hate
Push
Slap
Fight
Blood
Veins
Lying
Crying
Slowly
Man Crushed
Ego
Woman Hurt
Scream
Storm
Night
Wind
Calm
Shame
Guilt

"What Goes On In This House, Stays In This House!"

Sorrow
Forgiveness
Touching
Kissing
Love making
Disagreement
Argument
Fight
Blood
Hangover
Bitterness
Attraction
Admiration
Trust
Commitment
Betrayal
Disgust
Repetition

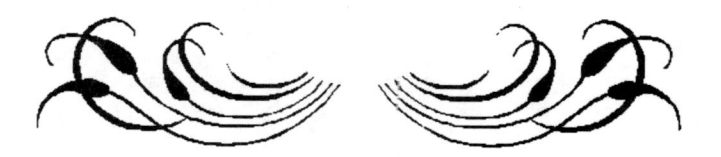

Tammy Woodard Rivers

Do You Feel

Does it make you feel
Like a great big man
Because you broke so many hearts?
Do you feel like a man
Knowing you left so many scars?
One day you're gonna miss my loving.
One day you'll miss my care
And on that day,
I'll feel sorry for you
Because I'm gonna laugh at you
And hope all the memories
Come crashing through.
I gave you all my love.
You stepped on it
And then threw it in my face
But one day,
Some day you're gonna be sorry
For the damage that you've done.

"What Goes On In This House, Stays In This House!"

MY PRIDE

I needed to scream
But could not,
Needed to cry
But would not,
Wanted to ask for help
But didn't know how,
Wanted to fall down to the ground
But feared looking like a clown,
Wondered why nobody was there,
Couldn't understand why nobody cared.
Should I have broken
Down and screamed?
Did tears have to fall from my eyes?
Did I have to get down and beg
For someone to answer my cries
Or did it have to do with my hair color red
Or was it me
And the things I should not have said,
Or what I should be
Or should not be
That brought no rescue to me?

Tammy Woodard Rivers

THEY WANTED BLOOD

They all flocked to see
Him rip out her eyes
And yearned to see blood.
Spewing from her soul.
Unsatisfied were they
To see him feel compassion.
They didn't care what she "felt".
Only wanted to see her moan.
Screaming, screeching agony
Is all that satisfied them.
Why would they stand around
To see him take her life?
No one cared to stop him.
They wanted to see life.
Life at its most vicious state,
Two humans with a gun!
Yet there was no gun,
Just two important people
Out to destroy
Where they had been,
Where they should be,
Where they should never see
In this human race.
They all stood there watching.

"What Goes On In This House, Stays In This House!"

CRY PRIVATELY

Don't cry for them sister.
Don't show them your pain.
A kick and a slap
Is all you will gain.

Don't you look down
And don't look to them.
All they see
Is the face of a clown.

Go find a quiet place
Where you can be alone
And that's when you cry
Of your unhappy home.

Don't let them see your frailty.
Don't let them see your weakness.
One day they'll look at it
As a sign of timid meekness.

Tammy Woodard Rivers

CAUSE I

*He left me
Cause I never did love him enuf
To let him hit me.
He hated me
Cause I wasn't about to let him
Misuse and mistreat me.
He cursed me
Cause I wasn't bowing down to "any" man.
He slapped me
Cause I'd never hit the ground
Down on "my" knees.
He punched me
Cause I wouldn't let him make me
Care less about myself.
He pissed on me
Cause I refused to sell my soul to the devil
By selling myself.
He loathed me Cause when I spoke,
I spoke in a whisper.
He strangled me
Cause when he looked at me,
He saw beauty
And all that any man could want.
He smeared my name
Cause he knew, that I knew
That he didn't deserve me.
He tried to kill me
Cause he knew
That one day,
I'd be
Gone!*

"What Goes On In This House, Stays In This House!"

"High Yellow"

He used to call me "high yellow"
Then he'd slap my face
Said he loved me,
Though he hated my race.

He used to call me "high yellow"
Said I was his prize,
Hated my superiority,
Detested my light gray eyes.

He used to call me "high yellow"
Before he'd knock me down,
Told me to crawl
Cause he liked seeing me on the ground.

He used to call me "high yellow"
On his way out
To search for a darker face
More "African", no doubt.

He use to call me "high yellow'
Because he admired and hated me
All in the same breath.
More than likely though, he hated himself.

For these same eyes,
Whether purple or green,
Could not have loved him more
Than if I had different genes.

Tammy Woodard Rivers

I'M NOT ASHAMED

Though I walk around
With holes in my shoe
And even with that laughter from you
I'm not ashamed, no I'm not ashamed.

My hair may be nappy
And I need a new perm
And the job that I work
Pays less that you earn

I'm not ashamed,
No I don't feel shame.
Though I was dumped at the alter by you
Told I wasn't good enough
Not fit to tie your shoe

I'm not ashamed, no I'm not ashamed
Ravaged, raped, tortured and denied
Kicked, punched and taken for a ride
But I'm not ashamed, I don't feel shame

Seen those around me
Who become and became
Watched them all sneer and smear my name
But I'm not ashamed. No, I don't feel shame.

Spat on, lied on, pissed on
Contrived against
But I'm not ashamed
No, I don't feel shame

"What Goes On In This House, Stays In This House!"

Clubbed in the head
Beaten and left for dead
But I don't feel shame
I'm not ashamed

Hungry, homeless, sick and decrepit
Old, gray, blind and unaccepted
But I'm not ashamed. No, I'm not ashamed
Cause I know my name.
And I know from whence I came!

Tammy Woodard Rivers

Lines On Her Face

Lines on her face she had,
Before the age of thirty-two.
Who would have thought life would
turn out so bad?
Who would've believed the undue?

Beaten way before the age of three.
Kicked and slapped mercilessly,
Reminded constantly of inadequacies.
Stumped, crushed and knocked
to the knees.

Raped, degraded and misled,
Loving only the color red.
Cuts, blood, shots, death and destruction,
All for the sake of the induction,
Into a life without a scheme.
Spat on, cursed, beaten, left for dead,
Torpedoed, bludgeoned and shot
in the head,
Yet still somehow able to survive.
Up mountain tops,
Down where the earth drops, she'd strived.

To suddenly awake from a nightmare
Wanting to believe what she saw
Was never there, could never be true.
Death by another name
Just doesn't seem fair.

"What Goes On In This House, Stays In This House!"

To survive and to live
And flourish and strive
To live from all which others must die.
That which isn't just,

To live with all she has, because she must
With lines on her face at thirty-two,
And pride in her heart
Because she made it through.

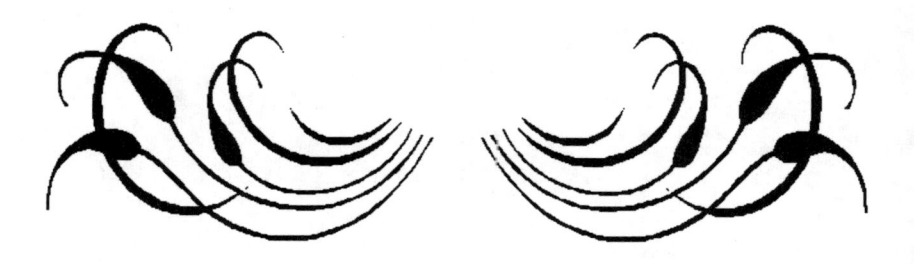

Tammy Woodard Rivers

I've Seen The Other Side

I've been on the other side.
I've seen the illogical
In the midst of logic.
I understand a kick;
I understand a stump
To the dignity of so-called love.
I felt love smack my ear
Until the sound of life
Was no more.
I felt the lonely rejection
Behind love's door.
I've seen the other side.
Yes, I've felt its reign.
I've held the hand of rejection, dejection
And oppression as it wiped up the blood
Of self loathe.
I watched the mutilation of my being
By the one whom I most cherished
In all this land,
In all the world.
I've seen the slap of degradation
Grow red then blue across my face.
I've seen the smile of life
Diminish and slowly disintegrate
And disappear,
As I became a degenerate of love
In its most brutal dance,
Love in its most hypnotic trance.
I've seen love.

"What Goes On In This House, Stays In This House!"

NOT SCARED ANYMORE

I'm not scared anymore
Too bad for you.
Loneliness, I don't dread anymore.
So sorry to say
Good-byes are on the way.
I'm not weary anymore.
I see tomorrow brighter now.
I know that I don't know
What's in store for me now,
But I'm not scared anymore.
Somehow I'll make the score.
I'll pick myself up
Each time I fall
And plant myself
On a more solid ground.
I don't need you anymore
I'm not the same girl I was before.
You see hurt and pain
Can blow you away
And yes, hurt and pain
Can send your dreams astray
But no matter what the outcome,
It's time I start searching for me.

Tammy Woodard Rivers

Life here with you
Is so sad and blue,
That even the unknown
Must be better than you.
No more crying in bed.
Time to face a new day.
I might work my fingers to the bone
But somehow I'll be strong.
Somehow I'll carry on
And I'm not scared anymore
Scared to walk out the door
Because, I want more,
And you're no longer
Worth fighting for.

"What Goes On In This House, Stays In This House!"

One Day You'll See My Greatness

One day you'll see my greatness
Suddenly shining through.
Someday you'll see my brilliance
Began when I left you.

Without you I found success.
Without you I found happiness.
Love envelops and surrounds me,
Something you would not give.

But one day you'll see my greatness
Suddenly come shining through.
I gave you all my love
But it wasn't enough for you.

How could giving myself
Make you want to hurt me?
Time waits for no one
And neither will I.

Tammy Woodard Rivers

No excuses please
For all the pain you conceived.
The day you see my greatness,
I feel sorry for you.

That will be the day
You'll see all you lost,
The day my brilliance
Comes shining through to you.

"What Goes On In This House, Stays In This House!"

HAUNTED

I let her have him because
She was better for him.
She could take the blows and kicks
That I could not take.
She could endure the scent
Of other women all over his body.
She could handle the unexpected phone calls
From his lovers claiming pregnancy.
She was a strong enough woman
To watch the candlelight,
As he cavorted with a new girl,
Wining and dining her on our electricity.
She didn't mind her children
Asking why their daddy is so mean
Or why she lets him hit her.
Going to work with cuts, bruises
And black eyes didn't phase her,
As the whispers followed her throughout the day.
She didn't seem to ache from sleepless nights
Of wondering where he was,
If he was in the arms of death
That resembles AIDS,
If he was outstretched on the ground somewhere
Behind police yellow tape
With a chalked outline drawing
Of the position of his body.
She could endure an existence of "whys',
Without asking why.
She never cared about
Owning, security, self-respect

Tammy Woodard Rivers

Or just plain sanity.
She didn't seem to feel
That her children's future was at stake,
As well as their dreams.
She did not see a better place, day, or time.
So, when she called me that last time,
I gave him to her
But I never expected him to KILL her.
Though her cruel voice over the phone
Crushed me on many a night,
As I cried bitter tears
Of how life ain't fair or right,
I never hated her enough
To want to see her dead.
Somewhere alone the way,
She got misled by love
And what it should be
And I can't help but to think
The same thing
Could've happened to me.

"What Goes On In This House, Stays In This House!"

AND SHE IS A PRETTY GIRL!

Her husband got caught with his pants down
With a prostitute on the back seat of her new car
And she is a pretty girl!
Her man cats around all over town
With anything in a dress
And she's a pretty girl!
He moved his woman in on his wife and children
And she's a pretty girl!
He beats her bad enough
To put her in the hospital
And she is a pretty girl!
He gives all of his money to a hooker
And won't give his wife a dime
And she's a pretty girl!
He's seen all over town with his mistress
And as for his wife,
She's a pretty girl!
He sleeps with women in her house while
She's at work
And she's is a pretty girl!
He had a baby by some girl cross town,
Even though he's been going with her 7 years
And she's a pretty girl!
He calls her every filthy name in the book
And she's still with him
And she's a pretty girl!
He sleeps around with men,
Even dresses in her clothes
And she's a pretty girl!
He pimps her,
Makes her sell herself to anyone on the street

Tammy Woodard Rivers

And she's a pretty girl!
He got her strung out on dope
And makes her do it with all of his friends
And she's pretty girl!
Pretty girl,
Tell me what you see.
Does being pretty not guarantee you dignity?

"What Goes On In This House, Stays In This House!"

THAT PRETTY GIRL

That pretty girl is going to suffer.
They all do
But people don't believe it.
They only see the world
Dropping external crumbs.
They never see the knocks and punches
That inevitably come her way
Or how far she'll sink to the ground
After living in the clouds.
They would rejoice
If only they knew what I know.
I used to be one.

I Didn't Cry

I was punched in the eye
By my brother
But I didn't cry,
Didn't even think it was normal
To cry.
Called bitch, dumb and stupid
By my brother
But I didn't cry.
Didn't shed a tear from my eye
Because I've had no other.
I didn't cry,
Couldn't cry.

Tammy Woodard Rivers

That Is Not My Brother

The worst brother a brother could have
Is a brother who calls me brother
Only because he is my brother;
Not because we are spiritually connected,
Not because he consoles me in return,
But just in "name" only.
That is not my brother!
One whom I must fight
Along with the world,
One whom I can't trust
With my most precious pearl,
That is not my brother.
That is not my brother
Whom walks a different line
And each time I get up
Wishes I stayed behind,
No, that is not my brother,
When the truth he will not tell,
One without a conscious of who and what I am
And one who uses the fact,
That he is my brother,
To demean and to destroy
Everything that a brother should be,
Like the brother that he found in me.

"What Goes On In This House, Stays In This House!"

I DRANK THE WINE BUT...

It was the first day
Of the twenty-first year
Of the happiest day of my life,
I thought,
When my brand new heart chose a friend
To spend my twenty-first celebration with.
We would drink champagne,
Dance and have a real good time,
Remaining the closest of friends.
Yes, he knew that I was in love with another
Who could offer me true devotion
And father all my fairy tale dreams
And it was okay because we were just friends.
I dressed in order to lure
And baited my hook with what would be
The most tasty treat I could contrive
to bring out the most deep-seated jealousy
In any man of pride.
In my mind I tantalized and mesmerized,
While boldly flaunting a scrumptious morsel
In the face of that which I most desired.
Yet, he would not bite,
So off I went into the night with my true friend,
Into what was to be
The savagely butchered mutilation of my innocence,
My trust and my self-esteem,
As I reached back in time
Again for my love over the phone line
With hope again
And hopes again of...
With hope again of...
Yet, no bite.
My friend needed to go to his house.

Tammy Woodard Rivers

He had wasted champagne all over his shirt
And would make a quick change.
Drowsily I awoke in strangeness, blackness
Hazily wondering
Who, What, Where and How?
Disgust, Contempt, Anger, Humiliation,
Frustration and Devastation washed over me.
In one minute second of realization
For the rest of my life,
I would be plagued by self blame,
Betrayal, RAPED on my twenty-first year of life
By a dear, dear friend,
Plagued for life by my dear friend.
I drank the wine
But did not agree to thine, not one time.
He butchered my trust and mutilated my self-
esteem,
Just as if I was a cow or a hog
Being slowly fattened and led away to market
To be cut up into various hunks for his enjoyment,
For his fulfillment, his worthiness,
his hunger and his greed,
Slice after slice,
Chunk after chunk,
My certain death.

"What Goes On In This House, Stays In This House!"

...BUT I NEVER THOUGHT HE'D RAPE ME

He picked "me" out of hundreds of girls.
Said I was the most beautiful he'd seen in the world.
We rode around town in his fancy car.
He introduced me to all the stars.

He bought me roses,
As we sipped champagne.
We went to a Broadway show,
Then down lover's lane.

He invited me to his classy hotel;
My friends, I couldn't wait to tell.
He treated me like a queen on the throne.
How could things suddenly go so wrong?

We talked til half past three
But I never believed he'd rape me!

He told me to stay overnight.
My flat would be fixed come daylight.
Said he'd be a gentleman and sleep on the couch.
But as soon as I closed my eyes, he pounced.

Thought I knew what he was about
But somehow through the night,
He slipped in and broke a promise
And raped me with all his might.

Tammy Woodard Rivers

I became lost that day
And part of me slipped away
For I had known him for over a year
And never thought of him as someone to fear.

I thought he was my true friend.
I just can't help but to wonder,
"What made him shed his skin?"

From that day to this
I'm no longer the same.
Never again will I trust again.
And never again, will a man be my friend.

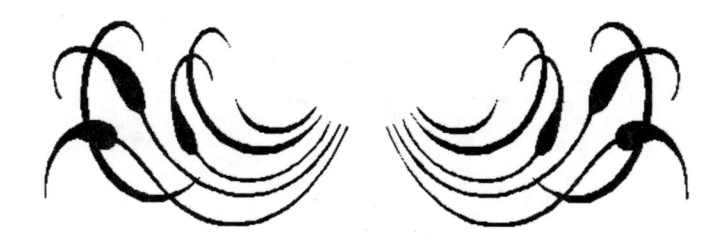

"What Goes On In This House, Stays In This House!"

Reminding Mother

I feel that I have to
Remind my mother
That my brother beat the Hell
Out of his child's mother
When she refuses to let him see his child
And what it feels like,
Since my Daddy beat the Hell out of her.
I feel she ought to remember
How it feels
To be guilty of only loving somebody
For them to want to beat you.

Tammy Woodard Rivers

YOU KNOW THE MOLESTER

The molester smiles,
Laughs and says, "Hello".
He donates to charity,
Goes to PTA meetings
And plays Santa Clause at Christmas time.
He gets involved in Neighborhood Watch,
Cares for the elderly
And is always willing to lend a helping hand.
He is the grocer down the street,
The Supreme Court judge, the school teacher, the minister,
The policeman, the banker, the baby-sitter,
The doctor, the nurse, the politician
And possibly even the President.
He is a superstar,
An astronaut or the winner of the Nobel Prize.
He can be a mother, a father, a grandparent,
An uncle, aunt, cousin, brother or a sister.
He can be your son.
He is sociable, kind, considerate and generous.
He can be a loving spouse.
He can be anybody.
He could be you or me.
There are no distinguishing scars
Or characteristics to look for.
He may have a house full of children,
And appear to be a dedicated parent
Or he may not have any children at all.
He may be a "she".
He may be your best friend
Or your worst enemy
But you know him
And you trust him.

"What Goes On In This House, Stays In This House!"

TO THE RAPIST

While you stand victoriously licking the blood
Of my life from your lips
And as you stand admiring your manhood
in the mirror
Of drunken brutality, I weep.
I weep for the part of myself
That you have destroyed.
The world to me
Has now become a battle zone
And I am its target.
Have you ever wondered
What I now think of you,
You who did not exist to me before?
You stand, not as a god,
But as filth that I so long to kill
That I even frighten myself.
I sit sometimes for hours
Planning your slow demise.
Joy only comes to me
As I, myself, slice out your eyes
And repeatedly jab your nose
With the longest, sharpes, jagged edged knife
That I can find.
I long to have to wrestle with the knife,
As it leaves deep gashes in your face, your cheeks
And the center of your forehead.
I long to hear your terrified screams
As I pour acid down your throat.
I'd even give you a cool glass of lemonade
To cool down your throat
So you can feel the knife
As it slashes, slashes, slashes at you Adam's apple.

Tammy Woodard Rivers

I am frightened by my cool rage
Because it longs to splice and splatter
The blood from your heart.
I'd save the best for last,
Your weapon of my destruction
It must be destroyed
And returned to where it belongs.
I shall first apply gasoline,
Then acid and finally I'd make several dices
To destroy that which destroyed a part of me.
I do not wish your complete destruction
For to die, you'd find relief and peace.
I wish for you a long life,
A life where I may periodically see you
And see that your suffering continues.

"What Goes On In This House, Stays In This House!"

THAT WOMAN DIDN'T MAKE YOU

"Mane, you oughta whup that bitch!"
Brother, brother don't listen to him.
Please brother, get far away.
He don't know what he's saying,

Don't know what he's playing,
A game of Russian Roulette,
Causing us all to behave this way.
I've got something I need to say;

We talk about the white man
And all that he's done
While we force our sister
To run with a gun.

She's tired of being whupped on,
Enslaved by the brother,
Degraded, frustrated, berated
And betrayed by her lover.

Can't you see what you do?
What if she did it to you?
If someone beat you on the street and
washed it down so neat,
I bet you'd sit down and contrive his defeat,
his last defeat!

Tammy Woodard Rivers

Stop beating the sister, like "Massa" beat
your grandmother.
Show some respect for all she has been
through.
Learn to protect another
Then watch respect shine back on you.

Educate your little brother
Give him an opportunity.
Show him a better life, of respect for himself
Because a world of respect is good for one
and all.

Stop degrading you mother
By whupping on your lover.
Stop taking away her freedom
to open up her mouth.

If what she has got to say
Ain't what you're about,
Be a man, stand up
And get the Hell out!

Hitting her in the mouth
Won't solve your thing.
She may not say it
But she'll play it again.

You won't change a mind
With a lick to the head.
So don't be a fool and wind up in jail
Or worse than that, DEAD!

"What Goes On In This House, Stays In This House!"

In jail you're put in a pen,
Like what they put animals in.
Knocks to the head and worse
Is the fate that you will curse.

Dead, what's left for me to say,
Except that you stay that way?
I'm not trying to intimidate you brother,
Just tell a little truth.

That woman you love, you say,
Didn't make you!
Stop and learn some respect for yourself
and what you do.
Slapping, punching or kicking don't make
you a man.
Understand?

Tammy Woodard Rivers

Friend To The End

There for me
Times I needed a mother,
There when I needed a lover,
There when I needed a friend,
There through the very end,
There when I couldn't
Be there for myself,
There when there
Was nothing else,
Oh you sweet
Tasty treat,
There for me
Whenever I eat.

"What Goes On In This House, Stays In This House!"

Part Five

Motherhood

Tammy Woodard Rivers

SUICIDE

Suicide was always the answer for me.
I knew that if things got too bad,
I would simply kill myself.
It wasn't until a child came along
That I learned to love myself,
To weather any storm
And to somehow continue on.
Now suicide is a thing of the past,
Though I sometimes remember when...
I now see the world
As it truly stands
And know that because I'm still here,
I'm a part of the plan.

BABY IN ME

**Just baby in me sit listening
To the peace and the tranquillity
While everyone else sleeps peacefully.
We listen to the peace.
"Thump, thump, bump"
Baby says to me.
"Where is everybody, Momma"?
I hear through telepathy.
Well I guess I'll go to bed,
Not too use to the quiet.
It's all very foreign to me,
Not such an interesting ride.
Kick!**

"What Goes On In This House, Stays In This House!"

Body of My Body Soul Of My Soul

My child,
I welcome you to this world,
And to you here and now, I surrender
All the love I have inside of me
Because child, I'm so glad to see your eyes
Starring back at me,
And your gentle grasp of my thumb
Reminds me that we are one,
Body of my body,
Soul of my soul,
Remind me to remember
That you are you.
I promise to protect you,
And to always love who you are.
I wish for you snowy dreams
Whipped in ice-cream
With Show White and Cinderella
And all those good things
That are purpledictome yellow.
I wish to you laughter
And Heavenly ever afters,
Unicorn wishes
And popcorn dishes,
Rainbow tickles
And raspberry icicles,
Cotton candy fun
And lots of basking in the sun.
My beautiful child,
I wish to you
A world filled with songs
That the angels sing,

Tammy Woodard Rivers

I wish to you luxuries,
That of a king,
Stars that kiss your sweet face
And I wish to you dreams
All wrapped in white lace.
Body of my body,
Soul of may soul.

"What Goes On In This House, Stays In This House!"

Deep Brown Eyes

Deep brown eyes,
How innocent they appear.
How very trusting!
So full of life,
Love and wonder,
So true and blue,
And weak and strong,
So real,
Those brown eyes
That I love so,
That I see in my baby's eyes,
Looking up at me,
Peering through me.

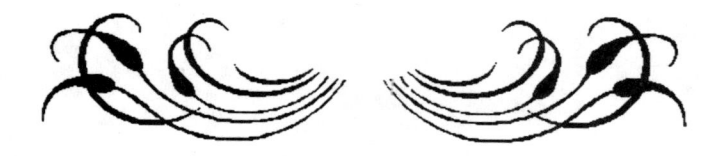

Tammy Woodard Rivers

WITHOUT MAKING A SOUND

Child of mine,
Sweet, sweet child of mine,
You've helped to drive a wedge
Between myself and my mother
As you showed to me
Through big brown eyes
Love true and pure.
Innocent and trusting child,
You opened my eyes
To forgotten pain.
You told me what you needed
Without making a sound
And showed me what
A mother should be
And all that I never had:
Always in your corner,
Always on your side
Believing, hoping and praying
While wishing the best for you.
A mother is willing to fight the world for you.
These things, I always needed,
From someone I never knew.
If only child I'd known you then
And all I know now and feel,
I never would have turned
The pain onto myself.

"What Goes On In This House, Stays In This House!"

HOW BLACK IS YOUR HEART?

How black is your heart
Beyond the locked door?
What secrets do you hide
Behind your disguise?
What lurid facts
Do you not want revealed?
What unsavory acts
Have you fulfilled?
How many have been sacrificed
At your soul's expense?
How many lies
Were told in your defense?
How black is your heart
Beneath its scars?
How many have been ripped apart
By the things you've done?
How much of your deceit
Will never see the sun?
What confessions will you make
In your dying days?
What unjust deeds
Will you take to your grave?
How many injuries
Have you inflicted?
How many sorrows
Do you hold inside?
How many casualties
Have you denied?
How black is your heart?
Hopefully not as black as mine.
Maybe next time,
You'll take a look at your own heart
Before you judge thine.

Tammy Woodard Rivers

I Am What I Am

What do you do
When you find out for sure
That a monster is part of you?
People tell you to forget
The past and all its' due.
Why can't they understand
That the past is who we are?
I wish I could make myself forget,
But I'm just an ordinary man,
And sad to say, deep inside,
I am what I am,
And no pretense can wash it all away.
What I witnessed yesterday,
Is part of me today,
And though I may dress it up
And sprinkle it around,
It always envelopes me
Whenever I sit down.
Those who came before me
and left as I watched,
Still live inside of me
And will til my clock stops.
Too bad I must admit though,
That one was a monster,
And though I deeply want
To forget that he ever lived,
All it takes is an explosion
And suddenly he reappears.

"What Goes On In This House, Stays In This House!"

IT COULD'VE BEEN ME

She killed her baby today.
It could've been me,
If a long time ago,
A prayer was not said for me,
By me,
"Please Lord, please, please God,
Don't let me do to my children
What he has done."
That baby died
Asking, "Why?",
"Why, why mother?",
Just as I do,
Just as I did
And now today
The Momma that loved her child to death
Is asking, "Why?".
Could've, should've, would've been me,
If God hadn't heard my prayer,
A long time ago,
When I was a child.

Tammy Woodard Rivers

A Mother Cries

A mother cries
For the loss of her child
Plucked from the core of her soul.
A mother cries
For the loss of breath
That she no longer holds.
A mother cries
As her body dies
For the life of her child
Is no longer inside.

MY CRUELTY

I wept today
For a creature of God,
That which is good, kind and love
Because I could not love it back
Or forgive it for less than he could
forgive me
And because I would greatly hinder
his chance
Of finding true happiness,
security and safety.
God, please forgive me.

"What Goes On In This House, Stays In This House!"

To Jennie

Jennie, don't take to heart
What I said yesterday.
Just remember love's flower,
As you run outside to play.

Momma never meant to hurt you
Or say things that are cruel.
Jennie, don't you realize
In my heart that you rule?

Try to remember always
Fireworks and tender kisses.
Jennie, I love you dearly.
It's for you that I make my wishes.

Try to bear in mind always
That I'm only a man.
Please realize my mistakes
But with a gentle hand.

Tammy Woodard Rivers

THAT'S MY DREAM

"Momma, I want to sleep by you."
"Momma, I love you."
"Momma, Momma, can I hold your hand?"
"I just love you so much, Momma.",
That's my dream.
I'm living my dream.
My child loves me
With all her heart,
Though there are moments
When she is angry with me.
I know that my child loves me.
Nestling up to me,
After sneaking in my bed,
That's my child.
Yes, my child loves me
But more importantly,
Of which I'm very proud,
Is the love I feel for my child,
Infinitely.

"What Goes On In This House, Stays In This House!"

Nobody Had To Tell Me...

Nobody had to tell me
That I needed help.
To feel the softness of my baby's skin
Against the coarseness of my sin,
Nobody had to tell me.

Nobody had to tell
That I needed help
When the anger cracked
And the lightening flashed
And the thunder rumbled and grumbled
And the house crumbled,
Nobody had to tell me.

Nobody had to tell me
That I needed help.
Nobody had to tell me
When the tears glowed
And the pain cascaded down
And the child wept
And my heart denied,
As my spirit cried
Nobody had to tell me.

Nobody had to tell me
That I needed help
As the memories crashed
And the darkness bound me
And the sickness surrounded me
And my heart reminded me
And my eyes betrayed me,
Nobody had to tell me.

Tammy Woodard Rivers

Nobody had to tell me
That I needed help
When the disgust lingered on
From the sting of my betrayal
On my hands and my fingers
And the memories of my mind resisted
The strange time, the moment,
Nobody had to tell me.

Nobody had to tell me
That I needed help
When the promises broken
Stumbled from my words spoken
Being down lifted
From being uplifted
To protect, to preserve and
To better humanity
Nobody had to tell me.

Nobody had to tell me
That I needed help
When the stench of lies
From all my Heavenly cries were denied
Nobody had to tell me.

Nobody had to tell me
That I needed help
When my hand betrayed my heart and mind
And the anguish lingered on in my soul
Nobody had to tell me.

Nobody had to tell me
That I needed help
When the stench of the abomination
Of the broken promises lingered on
In my nose, on my tongue
And down my throat,
Nobody had to tell me.

"What Goes On In This House, Stays In This House!"

Nobody had to tell me
That I needed help
When the sight of my child's lovely
soft silky skin
Caused fear in my heart and mind,
Nobody had to tell me.

Nobody had to tell me
That I needed help
When I realized
That I could not forgive
This same action
For which I needed to be forgiven,
Nobody had to tell me.

Nobody had to tell me
That I needed help
For I was the best authority of the situation.
I had lived the scenario through
And through the help that I sought,
I found that abuse is a vicious cycle
That lingers on through generations,
Unless you can admit and commit
to get help.
Nobody has to tell you
That you need help.

Tammy Woodard Rivers

SOON AS DADDY IS HOME

Soon as Daddy is home
We'll start our day.
I've got dinner cooking on the stove,
A chilled glass with wine on ice,
Soft music playing
And I'm smelling all sweet.

Children go to the window
And see if Daddy's home.
You know how much I love him.
It seems he has been gone so long.
I know you're anxious
To jump in Daddy's arms.

Oh, when he gets home
We'll have so much fun.
I'll go run him a tub of water
With a drop of his cologne.
You run get his slippers
And unplug the telephone.

Sometimes his day is so hard
And we should all just be left alone.
He tries so hard to hide it.
So children don't you fight.
Everything is gonna be all right
Soon as Daddy is home.

"What Goes On In This House, Stays In This House!"

PARENTS

Parents,

Please don't beat your children. You have no idea how much the blows will cost the child you love. You have no idea of the pain and suffering that child must endure for the rest of his life.

You don't know how much your grandchild will suffer. Some adult survivors of abuse can overcome their past. Most cannot. The suffering continues through the rest of their lives.

The most precious moments of that adult child's life can spark the most terrible memories imaginable. Nighttime can become such a difficult burden that the adult starts to resist sleep. The fear that overcomes a survivor is tremendous when discipline is necessary in rearing their own children.

Sometimes all the things that the survivor swears never to do starts to become the only alternative intellectually that the survivor knows.

Counseling helps but cannot take away the pain and is a long painful road. Some adults are too proud or too ashamed to admit they have problems. They must work that much harder to succeed at rearing and protecting their children or choose to never have them all together. Child abuse not only affects one child. It affects a nation. It is responsible for most of society's problems. What you do to your child is everybody's business. Your grandchild will one day walk the same streets, go to the same school and possibly even marry mine. I want a better world for my children and grandchildren than I had. Don't you?

Tammy Woodard Rivers

"What Goes On In This House, Stays In This House!"

Part Six

Survivor

Tammy Woodard Rivers

THE BATTLE OF MY LIFE

My life has been a battlefield,
As I fought my way to survive,
Up a mountain,
Down a hill,
Hoping to reach the other side.
Counting my every blessing,
For each small victory I could claim,
Wondering all along,
When it would all change.
Every time my name was called,
Silently I would smile.
I made it through another war,
Though I struggled all the while,
Wishing it would all end,
This dreary life I bought,
Knowing deep inside though,
A better life I sought.
Yes, I know it will never end,
This battle that I lead.
I guess as long as it stays this way,
I can't help but succeed!

"What Goes On In This House, Stays In This House!"

FINALLY ME

A long time ago,
I didn't know who to trust.
A long time ago,
I believed in you just.
Never took the time
To see who you were.
Never looked around
To see the wrong that you've done.
Wished I had the answers
To questions afraid to ask,
Never bothering to fight
And put you to the task,
Finally looked within me
And saw all that I was.
Now I understand
That I'm whom I should love.

Tammy Woodard Rivers

To Touch The Rising Sun

I never walked,
I always ran
To reach the other side.
In a hurry always
To see what I could see;
In a scurry always
To be where I could be.
No slow pace for me,
One so intent,
To see a life that's better
Than the life that I had spent.
No regrets for rushing
To touch the rising sun,
No sorrow for all
The races that I have run.
Many things I may have missed
With my fast pace.
The faster I ran though,
The more I met face to face.
I'd honestly say
By running all the time,
My life was extended
At least by ten times.
For even though I rushed passed you,
I slightly saw your face.
Who knows what I might have missed,
If I had slowed my pace!

"What Goes On In This House, Stays In This House!"

ON ME ALL ALONG

No longer a victim
By someone else's hand,
No more oppression
From dark Depression Land.

I won't feel guilt
From your lack of control;
No longer feel worthless
From something I've been told.

Deep in my soul I know
I'm an innocent bystander.
I don't deserve the treatment which
My life has based its standards.

I've been a slave all this time
Where my mind was the captor.
I've been alone never knowing
That I control my own rapture.

Sad to think all along
That I held the key;
Never knowing my freedom would
Someday depend on me.

Tammy Woodard Rivers

Saying good-bye to all the crimes
I've allowed inflicted on me;
Never realizing it's up to me
To be all I can be.

I now know it's not my fault
For the pain that I've endured.
This time in my life
I deserve to feel self-assured.

So many years I've lost
Believing I had no control.
So many years it cost
As I watched myself grow old.

Wish I could've found myself
A long time ago.
Where I could've been,
Is something I'll never know.

"What Goes On In This House, Stays In This House!"

SOMEONE IS MY NAME

Always struggling to be someone,
Hoping for the day,
Reaching for the sky
To find the greatness in me.

Wasted years and bitter tears
For something I could not fix.
Searching, wishing and hoping
To find it in time.

Wanting others to see
All I want to be
But somehow my interest never focused on me.
The problem was that I did not know
The trouble was with me.

Only I could determine
All that I could be.
Feeling from the beginning
That there was something I must attain;

If only I had realized then
That someone began
With my name.
Someone began with me.

Tammy Woodard Rivers

MY NAME

It's not a name that I'm proud of
But it was given to me.
I carried it
From as long as I can remember.
It calls itself me.
Many times I've wished to ditch it,
Pretend it doesn't exist.
I don't wish to be defined
By a few ridiculous lines.
People always promised
That no one could take it away.
How many times
I've wished to run astray.
I've taken others in to be my lover
But somehow they just didn't seem to fit
Which left me at my wits.
Many times I thought
Of choosing a stranger as another
But somehow it just didn't seem right for me.
To choose a name that I could not see.
Suppose it was worse than I'd want to be.
Finally after many a thought
Circled round my head,
The worst that I knew,
I could better myself
And make me who I wanted to be.

"What Goes On In This House, Stays In This House!"

SO THEY WOULD LIKE ME

I changed the hair and thought,
"Maybe now they'll like me."
But they didn't.
So I changed my occupation and thought,
"Maybe now they'll like me."
Well then I changed the color of my eyes
And even my dress size
Then painted my nails a ruby red
And changed the way I held my head,
So maybe now they would like me
But they didn't.
Then I changed the way in which I spoke.
Changed my habits to do dope
but still they didn't like me.
So I changed the address
From which I lived,
Bought a big house on top of a hill,
Started passing out dollar bills,
All so they would like me.
I aimed for a star and snatched down the moon
And placed it at their feet
So they would like me
But they never did.
So then I became ruthless.
I made the wind sweep far and wide
And ricochet back to me again.
I forced the snow from the sky in July,
Then made apple pie fall from the sky.
Yet they still didn't like me.
Then I took a look at myself
Trying to please everyone else
Made me dislike myself.
I finally decided to work on
Learning to like myself.
That was when I realized
That my best friend is myself
And they began to like me.

Tammy Woodard Rivers

Good-Bye

No more asking why
Things happen to me.
No more feeling guilty
For constantly being beaten.
No more sad stories
Of life as it could be.
No more injustice
Inflicted on me.
No more being a target
For anger's sake.
No more being used
Without being appreciated.
No more sorrow
For something I'll never have.
No more being pressured
Into thinking I'm bad.
No more wishing
That I could be you.
No more hoping
That you'd be strong.
No more thinking
That my thoughts are all wrong.
No more being
Anything other than me.
No more believing
That I'm less than everyone I see.
No more apologies
For just being me.
No more tomorrows
Wasted on thee.

"What Goes On In This House, Stays In This House!"

I Survived You

I won't hide or even dodge you
Because I survived you.
Maybe I'm not as young
Or as pretty as I used to be,
But one thing's for sure,
I survived you.
I survived your brutality,
Survived your evilness,
Survived your beatings,
Survived your vicious sharp tongue,
Survived your ego,
Survived your hatred,
Survived your insecurities,
Survived your insensitivity,
And survived your so-called love.
So why should I hide
From someone like you.
I hardly remember your face.
That's what I think of you,
I survived you.

Tammy Woodard Rivers

THROUGH IT ALL

*Through it all
I became.
Through it all
I survived.
I'm a woman
Just look at me.
I'm a woman
Prouder that you'd believe.
I'm beautiful.
I can do anything.
Through it all
I became.
Through it all
I still have my name.
I'm wonderful.
Through it all
I'm strong.
Through it all
I survived you.
Through it all
I can still claim
That I became.
Through it all
I'm still Sane.*

"What Goes On In This House, Stays In This House!"

I'M A TROOPER

I'm a trooper
I've been pushed around
And knocked down
But always got back up.
I've had to go on living
With those who squeezed my cuff,
Imprisoning me inside myself,
A person I don't wish to be:
Cynical, untrusting, pessimistic,
Believing only the worst of life
Because that was all I'd seen.
Somewhere deep inside of me
Buried in a dream,
I see bright colors
From a glorious day.
I dream of loving faces
Coming for me.
I see a life of hurt and pain
Washed all away.
I see a distant place
Smiling my way.
I'm a trooper.
That's why I go on,
Though I don't see happiness today.
Maybe, possibly maybe,
I'm just a breath away.

Tammy Woodard Rivers

NOW JUST LOOK AT ME

Look at who I am.
Look who I've become.
Boy, I'm so happy
For the races I have run.

Some races I lost right off.
Some I just gave up
But by always trying
Just look at the races I have won.

I just kept on living
And it all came to me.
I just kept on praying
Wow, just take a look at me!

Tell me what you see.
Tell me how you feel
And I'll tell you what I see.
I'll tell you what I feel.

I'll show you my pride.
I'll show you my love.
I'll show you my strength.
I'll show you my soul.

"What Goes On In This House, Stays In This House!"

Oh, how happy I am
To live one more day.
I know one day that I shall die
And I'm not afraid.

Just look at me.
Look who I've become
And remember always
What I started from.

Tammy Woodard Rivers

Blend In

Take the time
To look within your heart.
I know sometimes it hurts
When you feel your scars

But eventually they'll blend in
And be a jewel that you'll treasure
Because with the scars
Came a life that you survived.

Hold your head up high
And reach for the sky.
I know you can touch it
Because now it's in your reach

And all those that came and went
It's time to thank Almighty God
For delivering your soul
Through all those he sent.

"What Goes On In This House, Stays In This House!"

YET I BECAME

You gave nothing, only pain;
Yet I came.
I proved you wrong
And all you thought of me.
I held on
And found my own way.
Didn't allow you
To determine who I am today.
I realized a long time ago,
My potential and your limits.
So all I really want to say is,
"In spite of you,
And without you, I became."

Tammy Woodard Rivers

My Perspective

No more one-sidedness,
Seeing life your way.
Time for me finally
To choose my today,
Viewing from my own soul
That which is true,
No more constantly
Depending on you.
Won't criticize and interpret
Life from your perspective.
The time has come,
Finally come,
For a point that is objective.

"What Goes On In This House, Stays In This House!"

MORE LIKE YOU THAN NOT

I'm more like you
Than unlike you,
Though I choose not to be.
I still feel your reign
But now I see the pain.
Though I wish to not admit it;
Good came from you.
Your mistakes obviously
Gave me the clue.
And because of you,
Those that follow
Will have a fighting chance.
A man cannot live
Without making mistakes.
Just be strong and admit,
For God's sake
You were wrong!

Tammy Woodard Rivers

Yet I Feel

Though I no longer see you,
You exist in the cobweb corners of my mind,
In my thoughts and in my dreams.
Though I deny you
And refuse to acknowledge your presence,
I know you are there.
Though you may be a part of me
That I choose to forget,
You are a part of me
That I must always remember.
There is a lesson to be learned in your existence.
There is a lesson to be learned in mine.
Confusion, anger and frustration
Cloud my every thought of you.
I refuse to feel.
Yet I feel the love you had for me,
The love I had for you.
Intellectually, I can't process it,
Won't believe it's there.
Physically, I can't see it,
But I know it's there.
Spiritually, I know it must be touching me.
So long a battle,
So strong a war,
Never willing to end.
Before it's too late,
I think it's time
That we take control
And let each other in.

"What Goes On In This House, Stays In This House!"

DEAR DADDY

I know you've always wanted
To appear big and strong
But Daddy, didn't you know
That strength was admitting wrong?

I wish I could talk to you
About the way I feel
But you won't talk to me
On a level that's real.

You wanted to give me
The very best you said
But all your things helped me to see
That you've been misled.

Flowers, cards and candy
Are all very nice.
If only dear Daddy,
You'd stop and think twice.

To believe my love
Could be bought for a price,
Oh Daddy, I'm so sorry
But things will never suffice.

Oh yes, I want your love
More than I can say
And every day that I live,
The feeling won't go away.

Tammy Woodard Rivers

REGRETS

No one lives a life
Without making mistakes,
Without having regrets,
No matter what they say.
From the time I was a child,
As far back as I can remember,
There are things I wish I'd known,
Things I should have known,
Things I should have said,
Things I shouldn't have said,
And things I should have done.
Though several years have passed
From my first mistake,
I still can remember
As though it was yesterday.
I'll never take away
All the wrong I've done.
I live with myself
With my head held high,
With my chin to the sky
Because in the end I learned.
Now wasn't that
What I was supposed to do?

"What Goes On In This House, Stays In This House!"

Just That She Lives

I can't make her be
What I want her to be.
I can't shape or mold her,
No matter who she is.
Must always be happy,
Just that she lives.
Won't try to change or fight
A losing battle.
Won't sit and cry
And let my teeth rattle.
Know when it's time
To give up the fight.
Know in my heart
Who's really right.

Tammy Woodard Rivers

TO MOMMA

You stayed
And made your mistakes
And for that I admire you so.
Through all the rough spots
You overcame because you hung on in there.
I've always wondered
Just what you did
That made me always love you so much.
Now I know.
You hung on in.
Times you wanted to run,
You hung in there and did it your way,
The only way you knew how.
You taught me to be strong,
How to hold on
and always give to dawn.
You achieved as you hoped
Through all of your pain and sorrow.
You were strong and courageous
And for that you can be proud.
You gave me the courage
That I needed
to take care of my own.

"What Goes On In This House, Stays In This House!"

FULL OF PROMISE

Some graduate early
And find destiny very close at hand.
Others are left behind
And waste life unable to understand.
All had futures full of promise,
Yet most failed at what they wished.
Some stopped and re-evaluated
That which life chose to dish.
All summed up and divided down,
Life is what you make of it,
Take of it without a frown.

Tammy Woodard Rivers

IN FOR THE COUNT

No, I haven't succeeded yet
But there's one thing I can say;
I've always been in for the count,
No matter come what May.

I may or may not get there
But God knows I've tried.
It's not very easy with
These obstacles on my side

But I won't give up,
No matter what sorrow comes my way
I know there's still a chance for me,
That could come on any day.

As long as I remember,
There's something special in me,
I will succeed, so you'd better
Just let me be.

Maybe you don't understand
My pride and my devotion
And I'm sure you don't agree with
My unusual notions.

I don't ask you to understand
The different route I take.
Just wait and see someday,
The celebrity I'm gonna make.

"What Goes On In This House, Stays In This House!"

I OUTDID YOU, POP!

I outdid you, Pop!
In my house there is love,
Pure and innocent love.
We're bonded by love, respect, kindness and dignity.

We run, laugh, play, sing, learn and grow
In my house.
We rejoice when one returns from a day.
We wait impatiently for each other to awake from sleep.

We daydream about when we will be free
To spend the day, the whole day together.
We all feel sadness when one of us is sad,
Sharing life's frustrations, as well as its glory.

We share each other's hopes and dreams
We comfort each other's fears
And talk through our insecurities and disappointments
That life throws our way.

We delight in each other's spirit,
Coursing and pushing through
The true meaning of life,
Each and every day.

We are FAMILY, SOUL MATES and FRIENDS
And are not ruled by greed, money or power
But by LOVE, pure and simple
In the largest and most brilliant light.

I AM HOME,
Finally home
And we are one
In my home!

Tammy Woodard Rivers

I'LL SPEAK

I have a voice
And I'm gonna use it.
I have a voice
And I'm gonna speak.
No quietly sitting on the sidelines,
I'm gonna get out
And speak this true mind.
I believe my opinion counts
In what I have to say.
I believe my experiences spoken
Will make a brighter day.
I deserve to speak.
I deserve to shout,
So it's time that I get started
By opening up my mouth.

"What Goes On In This House, Stays In This House!"

I REMEMBER HEAVEN

I was taken prisoner
From the time I was a babe
Chained, whipped and locked in
Was where I stayed
Yet my soul remained free
To soar through the sky,
To float among the trees,
Denied the sun, the moon, the flower
Along with laughter,
I wished, dreamed and hoped
To see a nicer day,
Remembered from where I came
And all of the promises there.
I did not let faith
Fall from my eyes.
I did not cry about
All I'd been denied.
I remembered Heaven
And all that it was
And gladly took this job on earth
So I could be back with God.
I crawled before I walked,
And babbled so I could talk.
It's all connected
Don't you see?
Try before you fly.

Tammy Woodard Rivers

The Father That I Love

The father I know is old and wrinkled
Standing straight up to the sky.
The father I love never bothers
About my asking why.

He's warm and tender,
Sweet and plain
And smiles through the rain.
The father I love, loves me,
No matter what my name.

The sun begins to shine
Whenever he speaks my name,
The father I know and love,
Loves me just the same.

Through him I hear the birds
Singing in the distance.
Because of him,
I love my own existence.

Though he's not my own,
He is my father.
The father that I love
Never sees me as a bother.

"What Goes On In This House, Stays In This House!"

THE PERFECT FATHER

Few of you know
What I'm talking about
When I speak of the perfect father.
He is there to catch you
When you fall,
To wipe away your tears,
There to make you feel you're good
And to tell you that you can,
There when times are hard
And so are you
From touching the wrong side of life,
There to tell you, "Everything will be all right."
He's full of wisdom,
Enough to know
When to back off
And let you grow
But there just in case.
You really don't know
What a wise, wise man
He really is.
I guess he'd have to be,
To be Grandfather.

Tammy Woodard Rivers

Forget To Remember

We cannot choose to forget
Or choose to remember.
The memory is formed by the event
Whether good or bad.
No matter how hard we try
The choice belongs not to us,
Of whether to discard or to store.
Though try we may indeed attempt,
Failure we usually succeed.
Our subconscious picks up on
Each and every deed,
Good at times,
Horrific at others.
What's done is done
And may be in the past
Yet the mind will replay the tape
With the sharpest of pictures,
The most brilliant of lights
Where the minute becomes colossal
And every detail precise,
Or perhaps the opposite is true.
Sometimes our subconscious
Won't share with us,
What may have just happened to you.

"What Goes On In This House, Stays In This House!"

I AM

I am the crisp autumn leaf
Blowing vicariously through the wind.
I am that speck of sand
That seems to have no end.
I am the pebble
Whose uniqueness goes unnoticed.
I am the sun,
That chooses if or when to shine.
I am the night
That eases out the day.
I am the simplicity of another day,
For I know no other way.
I am the clouds,
Ever changing, Ever ending,
Ever, Ever, Never.
I am the birds
With infinite boundaries
And spiritual depth.
I am the oak that sees.
I am the moth that breeds.
I am the air.
I am nowhere, everywhere.
I am life's dare!
I am the calm after the storm,
The immaculate
After the Quake.
I am the cane after the Hurri,
The tame after the wild.
I am, I am, I AM!

Tammy Woodard Rivers

BOOK AVAILABLE THROUGH
Milligan Books
An Imprint Of Professional Business
Consulting Service

**What Goes On In This House,
Stays In This House $12.95**

Order Form

Milligan Books
1425 West Manchester, Suite B,
Los Angeles, California 90047
(323) 750-3592

Mail Check or Money Order to:
Milligan Books

Name _____ Date _____
Address _____
City_____ State ____ Zip Code_____
Day telephone _____
Evening telephone_____
Book title _____

Number of books ordered ___ Total cost .... $_____
Sales Taxes (CA Add 8.25%) .... $_____
Shipping & Handling $3.00 per book .... $_____
Total Amount Due...$_____

• Check   • Money Order   Other Cards _____
• Visa   • Master Card   Expiration Date _____
Credit Card No. _____
Driver's License No. _____

Signature   Date